# FAVORITE RECIPES

*from*

# Northern California Inns

*by*

*Dr. Ann M. Crowley*

Published by Crowley's Creations, 125 South Mount Vernon Drive, Iowa City, Iowa 52245

Layout, graphics and cover design by Susan DeSmet
Photography by Ann M. Crowley
All recipes selected and edited for home production by Ann M. Crowley
Cover photo props by Vanderbilt and Company, St. Helena, California

**Library of Congress Cataloging-in Publication Data**

Ann M. Crowley 2007
Favorite Recipes from Northern California Inns

Includes index
ISBN 978-0-9768139-1-0 (paperback)
     1. Bed and Breakfast/Inn information and recipes, 2. Directory of Bed and Breakfasts/Inns
     Favorite Recipes from Northern California Inns     Title

# *Preface*

The housing industry is a very old one. Ever since man first set out on foot, he has had to seek food and shelter. The shape and form has changed over the years, as have the names of these places of warmth and sustenance. They are called Inns, Tourist Homes, Resorts, Country Inns, Hotels, Guest Homes, Spas, Villas and Bed & Breakfasts.

In *Favorite Recipes from Northern California Inns* I have included the various types of guest housing that serve breakfast under the umbrella of Inns.

The Inns in this book are from Northern California and are grouped by the town where they are located. Each Inn has its own section. The information and history of each is found on the beginning page with the favorite recipes on the following pages. Page 240 has a map of Northern California showing a listing of each Inn and the towns where they are located.

A complete index of all the recipes in the book begins on page 241. Recipes are listed alphabetically under the food category as: fruit, meats, salads etc. Many are cross referenced. For example, a fruit salad would be included in the fruit category and in the salad listing.

The Directory of Inns includes name, address, phone numbers, and E-mail address and where possible, web page addresses. The names of the Innkeepers are also listed for each Inn.

*Favorite Recipes from Northern California Inns* does not include all the Inns in this area. It does include those who sent recipes, arranged for an interview and a photo shoot. The Inns described in this book provide the guests with comfortable lodging and excellent food. This does not suggest that the other Inns located in Northern California are less desirable.

*Favorite Recipes from Northern California Inns* affords the reader insight to the ambiance of the homes. The tested recipes make it possible to have a taste of the foods served at these Inns. I hope it will motivate the readers to seek the Inns throughout Northern California as a great relaxing and refreshing escape.

# Table of Contents

# Table of Contents

**Inns**

## Dedication

To my extended family, with love.

## Thanks

To the Innkeepers who generously shared their stories & recipes.

A very special thanks to Susan DeSmet for her dedicated help with design and production of the book and creating the illustrations. Without her help, this book could not have been completed.

And a big thanks to Mike Link who diligently proofed the material in the book.

# Introduction

I recently created a book of the recipes from the Bed and Breakfasts in Iowa and it was so successful that my family decided I needed to do a similar cookbook of recipes from the Inns in Northern California. In retrospect their support and the success of that first book should not be too surprising since considering the ambience of the Inns and the fact that food is my passion. In my career as a Registered Dietitian I have created menus, tested recipes and published three recipe books.

Using directories of Inns in Northern California, tourist information, the internet and telephone listings I was able to contact the Innkeepers in this region. In my letter to them I explained my project and asked if they would be interested in participating. Thirty five of the Inns responded and sent me copies of their favorite recipes. I reformatted each to fit the style of the book. All the recipes have been tested and those for large quantities were tested in versions that would be considered home size recipes. They are easy to prepare and will receive accolades from your family and friends.

The next part of the project was to contact each of the Innkeepers to arrange a time to visit the Inn, review the adjusted recipes and record the history of the homes. Four of the Inns in the book, Maison Fleurie, Lavender, Blackbird Inn and Healdsburg Inn on the Plaza are owned and operated by the Four Sisters Inns of Monterey California. They advised me not to visit their Inns and told me they did not have information about the history of their Inns. By searching newspaper archives, County records, library resources, historical society records, and visiting with long time residents in the communities I was able to learn the history of these marvelous old buildings. Scott Warner who rebuilt the Blackbird Inn was a wonderful source of information. The Four Sisters Inns were generous in providing their recipes for their Inns featured in this book.

The Inns that I visited ranged from small bungalows, to ranches, to large Victorian mansions. The history of how each became an Inn or bed and breakfast is fascinating. Many were built as a single family dwellings later to become an apartment building, a rooming house, a detention home, a restaurant and finally restored to its original splendor. Many are listed on the National Register of Historic Places.

After compiling the book with recipes, helpful tips, and the stories of the Inns, I again visited each of the Inns to photograph the prepared foods from their recipes featured in the book. The food pictures of the Four Sisters Inns were done in my studio.

Enjoy... I did!

## Foothill House

Although the house was build as a farm home in 1898 it does not look like a farm house. Many changes and additions have been made to the facility over the years. They are still going on.

In 1990 a large "cottage" was built up the hillside in back of the main building. It has views of the landscaped yard, water fountain and gazebo.

Doris and Gus Becket, both native Californians, are well steeped in the history of this North country area. They bought the Foothill House in 1991 after a lengthy search for the type of inn that would fit into their no-nonsense, unpretentious life style.

Darla Anderson, who purchased the Foothill House bed and breakfast just a few years ago, has been busy updating the home and the gardens. Much of the decorating was done by a designer in the Laura Ashley style. It is warm, comfortable and inviting. Darla felt it was time for an updating of the Inn. The rooms have been repainted and the window boxes have been removed and the balustrade railing redone.

The garden on the sloping hill to the highway has been completely redone into what Darla calls her "lattice garden". The area has white wicker furniture for the guests to relax on while they are viewing the flower beds and enjoying a refreshment. Often humming birds visit the flowers or feeders in the garden adding another attraction for the guests.

Darla Anderson enjoyed staying at bed and breakfasts but was not sure she wanted to run one. For her training she took a job at a bed and breakfast in St. Helena and worked there for a year and a half. This period of exposure convinced her that she really enjoyed the role of an Innkeeper. Darla told me she loves the guests and finds them interesting and fascinating. Many of the guests at the Foothill House have become Darla's friends. They return to the Inn often and it is not unusual for Darla to join them for dinner at one of the local restaurants.

## Broiled Blackberries

3 cups fresh blackberries
1 cup sour cream
1 teaspoon vanilla extract
1 cup brown sugar

Spray 6 ramekins with cooking spray. Divide blackberries and place in ramekins. Sprinkle with half of brown sugar. Mix sour cream and vanilla and spoon over berries. Sprinkle the remaining half of brown sugar over berries and sour cream. Broil 1 minute or until sugar caramelizes (watch very carefully).
Yield: 6 servings

## German Style Short Ribs

❖ *After ribs have been browned they can be cooked with all ingredients in a slow crock pot for 4 to 6 hours. They are very tender and the flavors will have blended.*

❖ *Suggested wine pairing - Zinfandel*

2 1/2 to 3 pounds short ribs, cut into serving size
2 tablespoons all-purpose flour
1 teaspoon salt
1/8 teaspoon pepper
2 tablespoons shortening
2 medium onions, sliced
1 cup red Zinfandel wine
1/2 cup chili sauce or catsup
3 tablespoons brown sugar
3 tablespoons vinegar
1 tablespoon Worcestershire sauce
1/2 teaspoon dry mustard
1/2 teaspoon chili powder

Roll short ribs in combined flour, salt and pepper. Coat all sides. Melt shortening in heavy large skillet. Add short ribs cook slowly until well browned. Add onions and brown slightly. Add wine, chili sauce, brown sugar, vinegar, Worcestershire sauce, mustard and chili powder. Cover and cook over low heat until meat is tender, about 2 hours.
Yield: 4 to 6 servings

## Oven Fried Buttermilk Chicken

1/2 cup parmesan cheese, freshly grated
1/2 cup wheat germ
1/2 teaspoon dried rosemary
1/2 teaspoon onion powder
1/2 teaspoon salt
1/4 teaspoon dried thyme
1/4 teaspoon garlic powder
1/8 teaspoon pepper, freshly ground
8 pieces chicken
3/4 cup buttermilk

Preheat oven to 325 degrees. In shallow dish combine cheese, wheat germ, rosemary, onion powder, salt, thyme, garlic powder and black pepper. Pour buttermilk in small bowl. Dip chicken in buttermilk then roll in dry mixture. Place on greased baking sheet. Bake for 50 minutes at 325 degrees, until juice run clear when chicken is pricked with a fork.
Yield: 4 to 8 servings

❖ *Bread crumbs can be used instead of wheat germ.*

❖ *Suggested wine pairing - Sauvignon Blanc*

## Almond-Tres Leches Muffins

1/2 cup butter or margarine, softened
2/3 cup sugar
1/2 teaspoon almond extract
2 eggs
2 cups all-purpose flour
2 teaspoons baking powder
1/3 cup (from 14-oz can) sweetened condensed milk (not evaporated)
1/3 cup whipping cream
1/3 cup milk
3/4 cup sliced almonds
Additional sweetened condensed milk (1/4 cup)

❖ *Can also be baked as six jumbo sized muffins.*

Preheat oven to 400 degrees. Grease 12 regular-size muffin cups with shortening or line with paper baking cups. In large bowl beat butter and sugar with electric mixer on medium speed until smooth. Beat in almond extract and eggs. With spoon stir in flour, baking powder, 1/3 cup condensed milk, whipping cream, milk and 1/2 cup of the almonds, just until moistened. Divide batter evenly among muffin cups (3/4 full). Sprinkle remaining 1/4 cup of almonds evenly over batter in cups. Bake 15 to 20 minutes at 400 degrees, until light golden brown. Remove muffins from pan to cooling rack. Cool 10 minutes. Drizzle 1 teaspoon sweetened condensed milk over top of each muffin. Serve warm.
Yield: 12 muffins

## Five in One Salad

1 cup fresh or canned pineapple chunks
1 cup mandarin oranges
1 cup flaked coconut
1 cup sour cream
1 cup mini marshmallows

In large bowl combine all ingredients. Stir to blend. Refrigerate for 1 hour before serving.
Yield: 5 cups

## Sweet Dream Cookies

1 cup (2 sticks) unsalted butter
1 1/2 cups light brown sugar, firmly packed
1 egg, room temperature
1 teaspoon vanilla
2 1/2 cups unbleached all-purpose flour
1 teaspoon baking soda
1 teaspoon cinnamon
1 teaspoon ground ginger
1/2 teaspoon salt
1 package (12 ounces) semi sweet chocolate chips
1 cup walnuts, chopped
1 cup powdered sugar

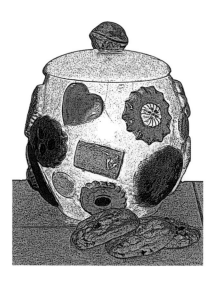

Preheat oven to 375 degrees. In mixing bowl cream butter and brown sugar. Add eggs and vanilla. In separate bowl combine flour, baking soda, cinnamon, ginger and salt. Blend into butter mixture. Fold in chocolate chips and walnuts. Break off small pieces of dough. Roll between palms into 1 inch rounds. Dredge rounds in powdered sugar. Place on greased baking sheets, spacing 2 inches apart. Bake for 10 minutes at 375 degrees. Let cool 5 minutes on sheets. Transfer to racks and cool.
Yield: 4 dozen cookies

❖ *Cookies stay fresh if stored in an airtight container.*

## Peach Melba

1/4 cup sugar
1 1/2 tablespoons cornstarch
1 teaspoon preserved ginger, finely chopped
1/4 cup butter or margarine
1 package (10 ounces) frozen peaches
1 package (10 ounces) frozen red raspberries
Sugar for sprinkle

❖ Two cans (15 ounces each) fruit can be substituted for the fruit in this recipe.

❖ Fruit can be poured into 8 individual ramekins in place of one round dish.

❖ Serve with whipped cream or ice cream.

Preheat oven to 375 degrees. Drain peaches and raspberries, save liquid. In saucepan combine sugar, cornstarch, ginger, butter and reserved fruit liquids. Cook over medium heat, stirring occasionally, until thickened. Add fruit. Pour into 8 inch round baking dish. Drop spoonfuls of topping onto fruit mixture. Sprinkle with sugar. Bake for 35 to 40 minutes at 375 degrees.
Yield: 8 servings

## Topping for Peach Melba

1 cup all-purpose flour
1/4 cup sugar
2 teaspoons baking powder
1/2 teaspoon salt
1/4 cup butter or margarine
1/4 cup shortening
1/3 cup water

In bowl mix flour, sugar, baking powder and salt. Cut in butter and shortening until particles are fine. Add water and stir to blend.

## Spanish Shrimp and Rice

1 1/2 pounds raw medium shrimp, in shell
2 tablespoons vinegar
1 tablespoon salt
Several dashes cayenne pepper
2 medium onions, coarsely chopped
3 tablespoons olive oil
2 cloves garlic, finely minced
1 cup tomato sauce
1/2 teaspoon dried oregano
Freshly ground black pepper
1 1/2 cups uncooked long grain rice

In large sauce pan place shrimp, vinegar, salt and cayenne. Cover with water. Cook for 3 to 5 minutes, until shrimp turn pink. Skim off foam from top. Drain shrimp, reserve liquid. Cool shrimp to remove shell and devein. Cut into medium-size pieces. In skillet, sauté onions in oil until translucent. Add garlic, sauté for 5 minutes. Add tomato sauce, oregano and pepper. Cover. Simmer on low for 10 minutes. Add rice, stir to coat. Add 3 cups reserved shrimp liquid. Bring to a boil, reduce heat and simmer covered until rice is tender, about 20 minutes. Add shrimp. Toss lightly with a fork. Cook 3 to 5 additional minutes.
Yield: 4 servings

❖ *Mexican leaf oregano has excellent flavor.*

❖ *Do not uncover the rice while it is cooking.*

## Mustard Chicken

1/4 cup Dijon style mustard
3 clove garlic, minced
1 chicken (3 to 4 pounds) cut for serving size pieces
2 teaspoons dried rosemary
Freshly ground black pepper
1/2 cup parmesan cheese, grated

❖ *Suggested wine pairing -
Chenin Blanc*

Preheat oven to 350 degrees. In bowl combine mustard and garlic. Arrange chicken in single layer in baking dish. Brush mustard mixture generously over each piece. Sprinkle with rosemary and pepper. Top with parmesan cheese. Bake for 45 to 55 minutes at 350 degrees until juices run clear when pricked with a fork.
Yield: 4 to 6 servings

## Grand Marnier Berries

❖ *Grand Marnier is a good
orange flavored liqueur to use in
this recipe.*

1 cup fresh blueberries
3 to 4 cups fresh strawberries, sliced
1 to 2 bananas, sliced
3 to 5 tablespoons sugar
3 to 6 tablespoons orange flavored liqueur
3 to 4 strawberries for decoration
Whipped cream
Mint leaves

In large bowl place blueberries and half the sliced strawberries. Sprinkle with half the sugar. Add remaining strawberries. Sprinkle with sugar. Drizzle liqueur over berries. Add sliced bananas and gently mix. Dish into individual fruit cups. Add dollop of whipped cream. Decorate with mint leaves and strawberries.
Yield: 4 to 6 servings

## Bear Flag Inn

*I*f you had a piece of land in Paradise what would you like to have on your land? Perhaps some fruit trees; apple, pear, nectarine, persimmons and quince. A big walnut tree for the nuts and the shade would be nice. Add a grape arbor for wine and a field of hops for beer. If you had a flock of chickens you would always have fresh eggs available.

I just described the Bear Flag Inn outside of Calistoga.

This piece of land has been part of California history. Enoch Cyrus and his wife Rebecca were born in Tennessee and gradually moved west, living in Illinois, Iowa and Missouri. They arrived in California in 1846. Their wagon train passed the Donner party between Truckee Meadows and the summit of the Sierra Nevada range. Enoch tried to persuade George Donner to cross the pass without delay, but the Cyrus party was forced to hurry on alone. They reached Sutter's Fort as the storm that trapped the Donner party began. Enoch worked in the Napa Valley for some years before he acquired the 200 acres in the upper valley.

Typical of the times was a certain social function that unfortunately lead to the untimely death of Enoch Cyrus and his two younger sons and nearly took the lives of his wife and young daughter. The affair was a wedding reception or "in fair" as it was then called. One of the guests coming to this function was a member of the Moore family from the lower part of Napa Valley. He was not feeling well, so when he got as far as the Cyrus home he stopped and stayed overnight. His sickness was smallpox. All of the family became ill and when it was recognized as smallpox the home was quarantined. Because of the fear of contagious disease Enoch and his sons were not buried in the cemetery but were buried on his land near the creek. Years later a headstone for Enoch was placed in the Calistoga Pioneer cemetery.

A young unmarried son, John, became the head of the household. In 1855 he married Lovina Graves. Lovina was part of the Donner party however she, her father, a brother and sisters attempted to walk out of the mountains. The Donner party tragedy took her mother, father, a baby brother and brother-in-law. John and Lovina had several children who continued to live on the Cyrus homestead. Descendants of these children continue to live on the property until 1986.

The Bear Flag revolt is associated with the Cyrus place. Peter Storm was boarding at the Cyrus place when the settlers revolted against the Mexican rule in Sonoma. He is credited in making the "Bear Flag" that was used as the flag in the uprising. Peter Storm is said to have been buried with his flag.

In 1986 an attorney from San Francisco purchased the Cyrus Sherwood property. He opened and operated a bed and breakfast for thirteen and one half years. He is also credited with planting the grapes on the acreage from which Cyrus Creek Cabernet is produced. Marge and Dennis McNay were traveling in their motor home and were looking a for place to park and a place for storage of their possessions. The Wishing Well Inn had been for sale for four and one half years and was quite run down. They purchased the home and acreage and spent the next six months renovating the property to restore the inn that they named the Bear Flag Inn. Now it is their paradise.

## Wild Rice Casserole

1/2 cup wild rice
1/2 cup brown rice
1/4 cup butter
1 teaspoon salt
1 can (10.5 ounces) chicken with rice soup
1 3/4 cups water or chicken broth
1/4 cup parsley, chopped
1/4 cup pine nuts

❖ For a low cholesterol product use Smart Balance instead of butter.

❖ The salt may not be needed in this recipe if the chicken broth is salty.

Preheat oven to 375 degrees. In skillet sauté rice in butter until it starts to brown, about 5 minutes. Add salt. In large sauce pan bring chicken soup and chicken broth to a boil. Add rice to boiling liquid. Pour rice mixture into greased 2 quart casserole. Cover. Bake for 40 minutes at 375 degrees. Remove from oven and add parsley and pine nuts.
Yield: 6 servings

## Impossible Quiche

4 eggs, beaten
1/2 cup baking mix (Bisquick)
1 teaspoon salt
1 to 2 cups cheese, shredded
1/4 cup milk
1/2 cup butter, melted
1 to 2 cups filling (spinach, mushrooms, bacon)

❖ Impossible Quiche is a heirloom recipe that was originally from South Carolina. It has been a traditional Sunday breakfast dish.

❖ Use cheddar, Swiss or your favorite cheese in this recipe.

Preheat oven to 350 degrees. In mixing bowl combine all ingredients. Mix to blend. Pour into quiche pan. Bake for 45 minutes at 350 degrees.
Yield: 4 servings

## Oriental Salad

1 pound bean sprouts
1 1/4 cups steamed rice
1 cup celery, thinly sliced
2 tablespoons green pepper, chopped
2 small carrots, finely grated
3 green onions, sliced with tops
2 cups cooked chicken or pork, diced
2/3 cup slivered almonds, toasted
Salt and pepper to taste
Juice of 1 lemon
3/4 to 1 cup French dressing
Lettuce
Soy sauce

In sauce pan cook bean sprouts in small amount of salted water until crisp tender, 2 to 3 minutes. Drain and cool. In large bowl combine bean sprouts, rice, celery, green pepper, carrots, onions, chicken and almonds. Chill thoroughly. Season with salt, pepper and lemon juice. Pour French dressing over mixture. Mix lightly. Serve in lettuce lined bowls.
Yield: 6 servings

❖ *For additional seasoning offer soy sauce with the salad.*

❖ *Suggested wine pairings -*
*Gewürztraminer*
*Off-dry Reisling*

## Creamy Scrambled Eggs

*Condiments to serve with the Creamy Scrambled Eggs are one half cup each:*
- *crisp bacon bits*
- *shredded cheddar cheese*
- *blue-veined cheese*
- *sliced ripe olives*
- *sliced green onions,*
- *small cooked shrimp*
- *caviar and sour cream*

*The Creamy Scrambled Eggs can be kept warm for as long as 1 hour on an electric warming tray.*

*For a unique and unusual brunch entree serve these eggs in potato boats.*

2 tablespoons butter
1 tablespoon all-purpose flour
1/2 cup sour cream
12 eggs
1/3 teaspoon salt
1/8 teaspoon white pepper
Parsley, chopped for garnish

In small sauce pan melt 1 tablespoon butter. Stir in flour. Cook until bubbly. Remove from heat. Add sour cream. Set aside. Beat eggs, add salt and pepper. In large skillet melt butter. Pour eggs into skillet, cook over medium-low heat. Gently lift cooked eggs to allow uncooked eggs to flow underneath, until eggs are softly set. Remove from heat. Gently stir in sour cream mixture.
Yield: 6 servings

## Caramelized Walnuts

*Continue to stir while syrup and walnuts are cooking.*

*There should not be pools of liquid left and all you should see are thick trails of liquid as you move the nuts across the pan.*

*Walnuts are really gooey.*

1/2 cup brown sugar
1/2 cup water
2 cups (1 pound) walnuts
1 tablespoon butter
Pinch salt

Preheat oven to 275 degrees. In heavy skillet combine sugar and water. Place on medium high heat. Bring to a boil stirring continuously. Add walnuts, butter and salt. Cook and stir until liquid is almost gone. Spread evenly onto cookie sheet. Bake for 20 minutes at 275 degrees. Cool.
Yield: 2 cups

# Huevos Rancheros

## Bean Quesadillas

8 flour tortillas
2 cups refried beans
2 cups Monterey Jack cheese, shredded

On one side of each tortilla spread a thin layer of refried beans. Sprinkle with cheese. Place another tortilla on top of cheese. In a large skillet or griddle on medium heat, cook the quesadillas until lightly browned on each side. Transfer to plate.

## Ranchero Sauce

2 cups salsa, any type
2 jalapenos seeded and minced
1 chipotles chili, minced
Small amount of Adobe sauce
2 cups black beans, cooked
1/2 cup cilantro, chopped
Salt and pepper to taste
Yield: 4 cups

In medium sauce pan heat salsa to simmer. Add remaining ingredients, except cilantro. Simmer for 15 minutes.

❖ *Prepared salsa from the grocery store can be used.*

❖ *Adobe sauce is available in cans in Latin grocery stores.*

### Cumin-Lime Cream

1 cup sour cream
2 limes, juice only
1 teaspoon paprika
1/2 teaspoon ground toasted cumin seeds
Salt and pepper to taste

In a medium sized mixing bowl combine ingredients. Mix until smooth. Refrigerate until ready to use.

### Eggs

8 eggs
Vegetable oil or butter
Cilantro springs for garnish

In skillet on medium heat fry eggs in pairs with oil or butter. Place eggs on top of quesadillas. Top liberally with ranchero sauce and drizzle with lime cumin cream. Garnish with cilantro sprigs.
Yield: 8 servings

## Peach French Toast

10 to 12 slices white bread, crust removed
3 eggs
2 cups half and half cream
1/2 tablespoon sugar
1 teaspoon vanilla
1 dash nutmeg

Arrange half of bread in bottom of 9 x 11 inch buttered baking dish. In blender mix eggs, half and half cream, sugar and vanilla. Pour half of the mixture over bread.

### Filling
8 ounces cream cheese
1 egg
1 teaspoon vanilla
1/4 cup sugar
1 can (16 ounces) peach slices drained

In mixing bowl blend cream cheese, egg, vanilla and sugar. Spread over bread in baking dish. Layer sliced peaches over filling. Arrange remaining bread slices over peaches. Pour remaining egg mixture over bread. Sprinkle with nutmeg. Cover and refrigerate overnight. Preheat oven to 350 degrees. Bake covered for 30 to 40 minutes at 350 degrees, until fully cooked and golden brown.
Yield: 6 to 8 servings

❖ *Less bread can be used.*

❖ *Be sure and saturate bread with milk mix. Add more milk if necessary.*

❖ *Sliced, frozen, canned or fresh peaches can be used in this recipe.*

## Deviled Chicken Wings

2 1/2 pounds chicken wings, rinsed and dried
1/2 tablespoon garlic, minced
1 tablespoon unsalted butter
1 tablespoon olive oil
1 tablespoon Dijon style mustard
1 tablespoon lemon juice
1 teaspoon Worcestershire sauce
1/2 to 1 teaspoon hot sauce (Tabasco)
1/2 teaspoon chili powder
Coarse salt to taste
1/4 teaspoon paprika
1 small red onion, diced or 4 scallions including green, sliced

❖ *Recipe can be doubled for larger number of servings.*

Preheat oven to 375 degrees. In large bowl, place wings and toss with garlic. In small sauce pan melt butter and oil over low heat. Cool slightly. Whisk in all remaining ingredients except onions. Pour over chicken wings to coat. Place chicken wings in shallow baking dish and bake for 30 minutes at 375 degrees. Reduce heat to 350 and bake an additional 30 minutes. Lightly dust wings with extra paprika. Garnish with onions.
Yield: 4 servings

## White Whale

❖ *Adjust the liqueur to taste.*

3 to 4 cups vanilla ice cream
1 ounce half and half cream
3 ounces Frangelico
1 ounce Kahlua

In blender blend until consistently of a milk shake. Dust with nutmeg.
Yield: 4 serving

## Bouillabaisse

2 onions, sliced
1 bunch leeks, sliced
1 stalk celery, sliced
1 clove garlic, slivered
1 green pepper, chopped
1 cup olive oil
1 can (16 ounces) tomatoes
2 cups vegetable or fish stock
Salt and pepper to taste
Dash sweet paprika
Dash cayenne
Dash thyme
Saffron threads
2 pounds hard shell crabs
1 pound red snapper, cut in cubes
1 pound halibut, cut in cubes
6 prawns
1 dozen scallops
1 Dungeness crab, cracked
1/2 small lobster, cut in cubes
1 cup Sauterne wine

Sauté vegetables in oil. Add tomatoes, stock and seasonings. Add fish according to time each requires to cook. About ten minutes for the clams, seven to eight for the snapper and halibut, five minutes for the prawns and scallops just long enough to heat through for the crab and lobster. Heat to serve.
Yield: 8 to 10 servings

❖ *Suggested wine pairing -*
   *Buttery-style Chardonnay*

❖ *The sauce can be prepared the day before serving. The flavors of the spices blend into the sauce.*

❖ *This recipe was developed in Portland and was used for groups and parties.*

## Chili Egg Puff

❖ *The top will turn golden brown and the center will be firm.*

❖ *Serve immediately while puff is high.*

6 eggs
1/4 cup all-purpose flour
1/2 teaspoon baking powder
1/4 teaspoon salt
1 cup cottage cheese
2 cups Monterey Jack cheese, shredded
1/4 cup butter, melted, cooled
4 ounces green chilies, diced

Preheat oven to 350 degrees. In medium size bowl beat eggs until light and lemon colored. Add flour, baking powder, salt, cottage cheese, Monterey Jack cheese and butter. Blend until smooth. Stir in chilies. Pour mixture into well-buttered 9 x 13 inch baking dish. Bake for 35 minutes at 350 degrees. Serve immediately.
Yield: 6 servings

## Cranberry Salad

❖ *This is a family heirloom recipe that was passed down from grandmother to granddaughter.*

1 1/2 cups fresh raw cranberries
1 package (3 ounces) strawberry flavored gelatin
2 medium size oranges
1/2 cup sugar
1/2 cup crushed pineapple
1 large or 2 small apples, chopped
1 1/2 cups water
Dash salt

Wash and drain berries. Peel oranges remove white membrane, dice, saving juice. Chop or grind berries and apples. In mixing bowl combine all ingredients. Stir to blend. Chill until set.
Yield: 6 servings

## Chelsea Garden Inn

The Chelsea Garden Inn really consists of two houses, a cottage and a guest room by the pool. The main house was build in 1927 and the second house some time later. The homes are craftsman style built with hardwood floors and wooden columns. This style home was typical in the early 1900's. The homes were generally one story and resembled a bungalow.

The two bedroom cottage was built in 1896. It was used as the home for the Station Master of the railroad. In fact, the turn-table for the trains was right in front of the cottage. He did not have far to go to be at work.

In 1980 a large second floor addition and an extension of the main building was completed. It included bedrooms, a kitchen, and a social area that opened unto the pool.

Joe and Lauren Scott bought the home 18 years ago and opened the first bed and breakfast. It was known as "The Scott Courtyard". In 2001 Dave and Susan DeVries purchased the bed and breakfast from the Scotts. They selected Chelsea

as the name for the Inn to honor of their daughter, Chelsea. The flowers and shrubs around the building and grounds fill the Garden part of the name.

Gary Venturi was the Innkeeper at the Chelsea Garden Inn and provided the recipes for this book. Gary has moved on and Connie McDonald is now the Innkeeper at the Chelsea Garden Inn. Connie has had significant experience in this type of position. In 1989 she was the innkeeper at the Guenoc Winery and Private Hunting Lodge. The hunters all had large appetites for three meals a day. For the past several years she has worked at several bed and breakfasts in Calistoga.

Connie learned her skill and love of cooking from her grandmother and grandfather. They taught her Southern Cooking. She has also taken cooking classes at several of the regional schools. She enjoys reading cookbooks.

While at the Inn, I sample the Inn's Signature Artichoke Spread and it was excellent!

## Vegetable Frittata

3/4 yellow onion, thinly sliced
1/2 large red bell pepper, thinly sliced
2 teaspoons olive oil
1 teaspoon butter
2 small crookneck squash, cut in chunks
3 small zucchini, cut in small chunks
1 head broccoli flowerettes, cut in half
1/2 teaspoon salt
1/8 teaspoon pepper
1 teaspoon Italian seasoning
1 teaspoon olive oil for frying
2 Roma tomatoes, seeded, chopped
1/2 teaspoon garlic powder
1/2 cup parmesan cheese, shredded
1/2 cup Italian seasoned bread crumbs
1/2 cup cheddar cheese, grated
7 eggs
3/4 cup milk

❖ *Suggested wine pairing -*
   *Chenin Blanc*

❖ *This dish can be prepared the*
   *day before serving and*
   *refrigerated. For servings cut into*
   *slices and cover with foil. Place*
   *into a 200 degree oven for*
   *45 minutes.*

❖ *For smaller servings cut into*
   *slices and cover with foil and*
   *place into a 200 degree oven for*
   *about 45 minutes.*

Preheat oven to 350 degrees. In skillet sauté onions and red pepper in oil and butter until slightly caramelized, about 20 minutes. Steam squash, zucchini and broccoli. Place in skillet. Add salt, pepper and Italian seasoning. Drizzle with 1 teaspoon olive oil for frying. Fry on high for 4 to 5 minutes. Add onions, tomatoes and garlic powder. Sprinkle with parmesan cheese and bread crumbs. Pour into baking dish. Sprinkle top with cheddar cheese. Whisk together eggs and milk. Pour over mixture in baking dish. Bake for 30 to 45 minutes at 350 degrees until set in center. Let rest at least 15 minutes before serving.
Yield: 6 servings

## Artichoke Spread

1 cup marinated artichoke hearts
1/3 cup mayonnaise
1/4 cup parmesan cheese
2 cloves garlic, minced
1/4 cup artichoke hearts, chopped
2 cloves garlic, finely chopped

Drain and rinse marinated artichoke hearts. In a food processor place marinated artichoke hearts, mayonnaise, parmesan cheese, minced garlic. Grind until well blended and smooth. Remove from food processor and place in a microwave safe bowl. Add 1/4 cup chopped artichoke hearts and chopped garlic. Place in microwave and heat on high for 1 minute.
Yield: 1 3/4 cups

❖ *Serve with toast triangles or snack crackers.*

❖ *This recipe can be doubled for a larger amount of spread.*

❖ *Spread will keep well refrigerated.*

## Pesto

3 cups fresh basil leaves, torn into pieces
4 large garlic cloves
2 tablespoon olive oil
1/2 teaspoon salt

Place basil and garlic in food processor. Grind to a pulp. Gradually add olive oil while food processor is running. Add salt. Adjust salt to taste
Yield: 1 cup

❖ *Parmesan cheese can be added to the pesto after it is prepared.*

## Peanut Butter Pie

### Crust
1 package (10 ounces) chocolate wafer cookies, crushed
1/2 cup (1 stick) butter
2 tablespoons sugar
1 teaspoon cinnamon

Preheat oven to 350 degrees. Combine all ingredients. Press into pie dish. Bake for 10 minutes at 350 degrees. Cool and place in freezer.

### Filling
4 ounces cream cheese
1 cup powdered sugar
1/3 cup peanut butter
2 tablespoons vanilla
1 cup whipping cream, whipped

*More peanut butter can be used if desired.*

*Smooth or crunchy peanut butter can be used in this recipe*

*Remove pie from the freezer 20 to 30 minutes before serving. Place each slice on the dessert dish for defrosting.*

In mixing bowl combine cheese and sugar. Add peanut butter and vanilla. Fold in whipped cream. Pour mixture into pie crust. Place in freezer.

### Chocolate Topping
2 squares (2 ounces) unsweetened chocolate.
1/2 cup sugar
1 tablespoon butter
1 can (2/3 cup) evaporated milk

Melt chocolate over hot water. Stir in sugar and butter. Slowly add evaporated milk. Cook until thickened, stirring occasionally. Cool completely. Spread over pie.
Yield: 6 to 8 servings

# Pumpkin Cheesecake

## Crust
1 1/2 cups graham cracker crumbs
1/3 cup sugar
6 tablespoons butter, melted

In medium size bowl combine all ingredients for crust. Press into bottom and 1 inch up sides of spring form cake pan

## Filling
3 packages (8 ounces each) cream cheese
3/4 cup sugar
3/4 cup firmly packed light brown sugar
5 eggs
1 can (16 ounces) pumpkin
1 3/4 teaspoons pumpkin pie spice
1/4 cup whipping cream

Preheat oven to 325 degrees. In a large mixing bowl beat cream cheese on medium speed until smooth. Add sugars gradually, beating until well mixed. Beat in eggs one at a time, until mixture is light and fluffy. Beat in pumpkin, pumpkin pie spice and cream at low speed. Pour into crust in spring form pan. Bake for 1 hour and 35 minutes at 325 degrees. Remove cake from oven and sprinkle with walnut topping. Bake an additional 10 minutes Cool cake on wire rack. Refrigerate for several hours or overnight
Yield: 12 to 16 servings

## Walnut topping
6 tablespoons butter, softened
1 cup firmly packed brown sugar
1 cup walnuts, chopped.

In a small bowl, combine butter and sugar until crumbly. Blend in walnuts.
Yield: 2 cups

## Crostini with Tomato, Basil and Feta

1 baguette, sliced
2 tablespoons extra virgin olive oil
1/2 teaspoon salt
1/2 teaspoon garlic powder
5 Roma tomatoes, chopped
1/2 cup yellow onion, finely chopped
2 tablespoon pesto
Salt and garlic powder to taste
1/4 cup feta cheese, crumbled
3 to 4 leaves fresh basil

❖ *Feta cheese with tomato and basil makes a nice topping.*

❖ *If the baguettes will not be served right away after they are prepared spread a thin layer of cream cheese over the baguette before putting the tomato mixture on the baguette*

Preheat oven to 350 degrees. Brush sliced baguette with olive oil. Sprinkle with salt and garlic powder. Bake until firm to touch in 350 degree oven. In bowl combine tomatoes, onions and pesto. Add salt and garlic powder to taste. Spoon mixture onto baguette slices. Top with feta cheese. Roll basil leaves and slice. Place strips on top of cheese.
Yield: 25 to 30 crostini slices

## Persimmon Cookies

1/2 cup butter
1 cup sugar
1 egg
1 cup persimmon pureé
2 cups all-purpose flour
2 teaspoons baking powder
1/2 teaspoon baking soda
1/2 teaspoon cinnamon
1/2 teaspoon nutmeg
1/2 teaspoon salt
1/2 teaspoon cloves, ground
1 cup nuts, chopped

Preheat oven to 350 degrees. In mixing bowl cream butter and sugar. Add egg, persimmon pureé, flour, baking powder, baking soda and spices. Mix well. Drop by teaspoon onto greased cookie sheet. Bake for 10 to 12 minutes at 350 degrees.
Yield: 5 dozen cookies

❖ *3 medium or 2 large persimmons make 1 cup puree.*

❖ *Adding nuts is optional.*

❖ *All types of nuts can be used in this recipe, if desired.*

# Rabbit Cacciatore

1 rabbit, cut into serving size pieces
1/2 cup all-purpose flour
1 teaspoon salt
1/2 teaspoon black pepper
2 tablespoons olive oil
1 1/2 large onions, chopped
1/4 cup fresh parsley, chopped
2 sprigs fresh rosemary, chopped or 1 teaspoon dried rosemary
1 green bell pepper chopped or 1 red bell pepper, chopped
2 tablespoon fresh thyme, chopped or 1 teaspoon dried thyme
8 cloves garlic, chopped
1 large tomato, skinned and chopped
2 tablespoons fresh basil, chopped or 1 tablespoon pesto
Water as needed
3/4 to 1 cup white wine

*❖ This recipe came from Gary's grandmother, NoNa, who owned a restaurant in Ukiah.*

*❖ Suggested wine pairing - Chianti*

Combine flour, salt and pepper. Coat rabbit pieces with mixture. Heat oil in large skillet. Brown rabbit in hot oil. Add onions, parsley and bell pepper. Cook until soft. Add rosemary, thyme and garlic. Cook for 3 minutes stirring occasionally. Transfer rabbit and mixture to large pot. Add tomato and basil. Place 1/2 inch of water into the skillet used for cooking the rabbit. Scrape the drippings. Add to rabbit in the pot. Add water to cover rabbit and mixture in the pot. Add wine. Cover and simmer on top of the stove for 1 hour until rabbit is tender.
Yield: 8 servings

## Brannon Cottage Inn

Sam Brannan became one of the first millionaires in California. He came by boat from New York to Yerba Buena, later renamed San Francisco. He was into everything that would make money. When gold was discovered, he found his "gold" by selling supplies to the miners. As his wealth grew he looked for more opportunities. Sam had heard about the hot springs north of Napa where wealthy people went for their health benefits. He made his way to the hot springs and by 1850 was extolling his dream of creating a "Saratoga of California".

Sam Brannan not only developed Calistoga, California but is credited with naming the town. In an attempt to say "the Saratoga of California," after a few drinks, he uttered Calistoga of Sarafornia.

Sam Brannan's resort opened in Calistoga in 1859 with an up-scale hotel and 25 cottages; each with five rooms. Each cottage had a wide porch with scalloped trim along the eaves. Others had mansard roofs and gingerbread decorations. The cottages were placed in a wide circular avenue on either side of Calistoga's main street.

Little is known of the Brannon Cottages from 1890 to 1984. By this time they were run down. Some were being used as farm worker's housing, some had been demolished and others were in ruins. The Indian Springs Spa bought the land and cottages. The cottages were scheduled to be torn down, however the decendents of Sam Brannan bought two of the cottages. They restored the cottages to their 1860 glory and had them listed on the National Register of Historic Places. One cottage, at 109 Wapoo Avenue became a bed and breakfast inn and the other one was moved to the museum in Calistoga, where it can be seen today.

In 2004, Judy and Doug Cook finally realized their dream of owning a bed and breakfast. Throughout 29 years of marriage, they had visited many bed and breakfasts around the country. When they started looking to buy a bed and breakfast, they considered Chicago, Oregon and Arizona. In California they explored Sonoma, Mendocino and Napa Counties. The Brannan Cottage Inn was just what they had been looking for.

Running the Inn was a natural for Judy who had significant experience cooking for her four sons and their friends, who where always happy to stay for dinner and often stayed for breakfast as well!

## Apple Oven Pancake

**Batter**
3/4 cup milk
3/4 cup all-purpose flour
5 medium size eggs
1 1/2 teaspoons baking soda

In mixing bowl combine all ingredients. Beat on high speed until smooth.

**Filling**
3 Granny Smith apples, peeled and sliced
1/4 cup butter
1/4 cup sugar
1 teaspoon cinnamon
1/2 teaspoon nutmeg

**Topping**
1/4 sugar
1 teaspoon cinnamon
1 tablespoon butter, melted

❖ *Slice into wedges.*

❖ *Garnish with sour cream.*

Preheat oven to 400 degrees. Sauté apples with butter, sugar, cinnamon and nutmeg. Pour into 8-inch square baking dish. Pour batter over apples. Bake for 10 minutes at 400 degrees. Remove from oven and add topping. Return to oven for 20 minutes.
Yield: 6 serving

## Sierra Dip

1 cup mayonnaise
1 cup sour cream
1 1/2 tablespoons green onions, minced
1 1/2 tablespoons parsley, finely chopped
1/2 tablespoon dill weed

❖ *The dip is better after flavors blend when held in the refrigerator.*

In medium size bowl mix all ingredients to blend. Refrigerate for 4 hours before serving.
Yield: 2 1/4 cups

## Shish Kabob with Seasoned Rice

1 package (6 ounces) long grain and wild rice
1/2 cup mayonnaise
2 cups mushrooms, sliced
1 pound lamb, cut in 1 1/2 inch cubes
1 cup cherry tomatoes
1/2 cup green pepper chunks

Preheat oven to 350 degrees. Prepare rice according to directions on package omitting margarine. In bowl combine rice, mayonnaise and mushrooms. Toss lightly. Spoon into 10 x 6 inch baking dish. Alternate meat, tomatoes and green pepper on 4 skewers. Arrange skewers over rice. Bake for 40 minutes at 350 degrees.
Yield: 4 servings

## Shish Kabob Sauce

1/2 cup mayonnaise
2 tablespoons parsley, chopped
2 tablespoons onions, chopped
1 tablespoon milk
1/4 teaspoon salt
1/8 teaspoon garlic powder
1/8 teaspoon black pepper

In bowl combine all ingredients. Mix well. Serve with kabobs.

❖ *Red and yellow sweet peppers can be added on the skewers for more color.*

❖ *A fresh mushroom on the end of the skewer is a nice crown for the kabob.*

❖ *The juice from the meat and vegetables during cooking adds flavor to the rice.*

❖ *Sauce can be served along with the kabob or drizzled over the meat.*

## Banana Bread

1/2 cup butter flavored shortening
1 cup sugar
2 eggs
3 ripe bananas, mashed
2 cups all-purpose flour
1 teaspoon baking soda

❖ *This banana bread is known as Judy's Banana Bread.*

Preheat oven to 350 degrees. In mixing bowl mix shortening, sugar and eggs. Add bananas. Mix well. Add flour and baking soda. Stir to blend. Pour into greased loaf pan. Bake for 60 minutes at 350 degrees, until wooden pick inserted in center comes out clean.
Yield: 10 to 12 servings

## Guest Pancakes

❖ *This recipe is known as Greg and Anne's Guest Pancakes.*

❖ *If you prefer a sweeter pancake add more sugar.*

❖ *Add water for desired thickness of batter.*

❖ *These generally cook at a slightly lower temperature for slightly longer because they are generally thicker than normal pancakes.*

1 1/4 cups all-purpose flour
1/4 cup toasted wheat germ
1 1/2 tablespoons sugar
1 teaspoon salt
1 1/2 teaspoons baking powder
1 teaspoon baking soda
2 cups plain low fat yogurt
2 eggs
1/4 cup vegetable oil
3 tablespoons water

In mixing bowl combine flour, wheat germ, sugar, salt, baking powder and baking soda. In separate bowl combine yogurt, eggs, oil and water. Pour liquid mixture into dry ingredients. Mix to blend. Ladle onto medium hot griddle. When bubbles appear on top turn to cook other side.
Yield: 4 to 6 servings

## Beef and Vegetable Torte

3 to 4 small (1 pound) zucchini
1/2 cup onion, chopped
1/4 cup vermouth
1 pound lean ground beef
1 package (10 ounces) chopped frozen spinach, cooked, drained
2 eggs, beaten
1/4 cup evaporated milk
1/2 cup dry bread crumbs, finely chopped
2/3 cup parmesan cheese, grated
1 clove garlic, chopped
1/4 teaspoon rosemary
1/4 teaspoon oregano
Pinch allspice
Seasoned pepper to taste

Preheat oven to 350 degrees. Wash zucchini and trim ends. Cook whole in boiling salted water for 10 minutes or until tender. Drain, chop coarsely and drain again. In skillet combine onions and vermouth. Cook over medium heat until steamy, stirring. Cover. Reduce heat to low. Cook 5 minutes, until onion is tender and wine has evaporated. Remove onion from pan. In sauce pan sauté beef until no longer red, stirring with fork to separate. Drain meat thoroughly. Combine meat, onion and zucchini. Add all remaining ingredients, except 2 tablespoons cheese. Spoon mixture into 9 inch pie plate. Smooth top. Sprinkle with remaining cheese. Bake for 45 minutes at 350 degrees, until wooden pick inserted in center comes out clean. Let stand in warm place for 10 to 15 minutes before cutting.
Yield: 4 to 6 servings

❖ *This torte can be prepared a day before serving and refrigerated over night.*

❖ *Beef Vegetable Torte is simple to prepare for a crowd. It is a hit at a pot luck supper.*

❖ *Suggested wine pairing - Pinot Noir*

## Barrett's Chili

❖ *This is a favorite recipe of Judy's friend named Barrett.*

❖ *Barrett's Chili is a popular dish with children of all ages.*

2 1/2 pounds boneless beef chuck steak, cut into cubes
1 tablespoon garlic flavored oil
1 can (29 ounces) pinto beans
1 can (29 ounces) chili beans
1 can (15 ounces) kidney beans, drained
1 package (1 ounce) chili seasoning
1 can (15 ounces) tomato sauce
1 can (16 ounces) tomatoes, drained
1 onion, chopped
1/2 cup cheddar cheese, shredded for garnish

In skillet brown meat in oil. In large pot combine all ingredients, except cheese. Bring to a boil. Reduce heat to simmer for 2 1/2 hours. Garnish with cheddar cheese.
Yield: 10 servings

## Adagio Inn

*T*he exact date of construction for this historic Queen Anne cottage in St. Helena, California has not been discovered. It does not appear on the Sanborn Fire Insurance map of St. Helena in 1899. The earliest record of any one living here is that of Walter and Susan Metzner who bought the property including the land at the corner of Kearney and Adams Street. They lived in the house at 1407 Kearney until the completion of their home in 1905.

The Queen Anne cottage has a hip roof and square bay windows on the right front side of the home. This was typical of the Victorian homes Eastlake effect at the turn of the century. The wrap-around porch has a "saw cut" balustrade or railing and Colonial revival columns. The house was built with three bedrooms, kitchen, dining room, living room and home office. The original wainscoting and moldings are in the present kitchen that once was the dining room. The James Beards lived in the home from 1945 to 1961, renting first from the Metzger's and then the Bullets. They reversed the bedrooms and living room.

Over the years additions and changes have been made to the home. Mr. Russ Burr, a building contractor, bought the house in 1967. He added the inside arch, beveled glass and the hardwood floors.

Originally the house had a large basement. This made it possible for Claudia Chestelson the new owner, to have the house raised five feet to install a full first floor. Valley Architects designed the project and worked with the construction crew to raise the house. This enlarged the house to five bedrooms, five full bathrooms, a living room, dining room and kitchen. Claudia opened a bed and breakfast. The home was known as the Chestelson House.

Paulette "Polly" Keegan is the present owner of the home now called the Adagio Inn. Polly lived in New York and when she completed her project at Columbia University the opportunity came for her to make a career change. She thought about becoming the operator of a bed and breakfast and found one in South Carolina that interested her. Just for curiosity she went on the internet to see what jobs might be available. A position in the academic field in a collage in the Napa Valley was listed. Polly decided to check it out and came to the wine country of California. With the help of a local real estate agent she found the bed and breakfast that met her needs in St. Helena.

Polly has made several changes in the Inn. The bedrooms have been converted into three large suites. She has built a comfortable living area for herself on the first level adjacent to the gardens.

## Heirloom Tomato Quiche

1 9-inch pie crust, unbaked
3/4 cup parmesan cheese, shredded
3/4 cup green onions, chopped
3 heirloom tomatoes
2 tablespoons all-purpose flour
Salt and pepper
1/2 cup fresh mushrooms, quartered
2 eggs
1/2 cup half and half cream

Preheat oven to 400 degrees. Sprinkle pie crust with 2 tablespoons cheese and half the onions. Cut tomatoes into chunks. Roll in flour. Place tomatoes in pie crust. Sprinkle with salt and pepper. Put half the remaining cheese on tomatoes. Add mushrooms and remaining onion. In bowl beat eggs and cream. Pour over tomato mixture. Sprinkle with remaining cheese. Bake for 35 to 40 minutes at 400 degrees.
Yield: 6 servings

## Basic Scones

❖ *For apple scones add 1 cup chopped apples and 1/2 teaspoon cinnamon to dough.*

❖ *For orange chocolate chip scones add zest of one orange, 1 cup chopped, drained mandarin oranges, 1/2 teaspoon orange extract and 1 cup chocolate chips.*

2 cups all-purpose flour
1/2 cup sugar
1/2 teaspoon baking powder
1/2 teaspoon baking soda
1/4 teaspoon salt
1/2 cup cold margarine or butter, cut into small chunks
1/2 cup buttermilk
1/4 teaspoon vanilla
1 egg white, lightly beaten

Preheat oven to 400 degrees. In food processor combine first 6 ingredients. Place in large bowl. Add buttermilk and vanilla. Mix until moistened. Turn dough onto floured surface. Knead 4 or 5 times. Shape dough into 8-inch circle. Place on greased pan. Cut dough into 8 wedges. Brush with egg white. Sprinkle with sugar. Bake for 18 minutes.
Yield: 8 scones

## Sausage Cups with Soft Scrambled Eggs

### Sausage Cups
1 pound bulk pork sausage
1 tablespoon onions, chopped
2/3 cup rolled oats
1 egg white
1/4 cup milk

Preheat oven to 350 degrees. In mixing bowl combine all ingredients. Mix. Divide into greased muffin cups or custard cups. Bake for 12 to 15 minutes at 350 degrees. Drain excess fat, keep warm. Fill each cup with scrambled eggs.
Yield: 4 to 6 servings

### Scrambled Eggs
2 tablespoons scallions
1 tablespoon butter
1/2 cup cream cheese
8 eggs, slightly beaten
Salt and pepper
3/4 cup fresh tomatoes, seeded, chopped

In skillet sauté scallions in butter. Add cream cheese. Stir. Add eggs, salt and pepper. Cook to desired consistency. Add tomatoes. Serve in sausage cups.
Yield: 4 to 6 servings

❖ *If possible use heirloom tomatoes.*

❖ *Suggested wine pairings -*
  *Moscato*
  *White Zinfandel*

## Spinach Artichoke Cheese Custard

6 large eggs
1 cup cottage cheese
1 cup Monterey Jack cheese, shredded
1/4 cup parmesan cheese, shredded
1/8 teaspoon ground mustard
1/4 teaspoon salt
1/4 teaspoon nutmeg
1 cup canned artichoke hearts, quartered
1 cup frozen spinach chopped, thawed

❖ *Ricotta cheese may be substituted for cottage cheese.*

Preheat oven to 350 degrees. In mixing bowl blend eggs, cottage cheese, 1/2 cup Monterey Jack cheese, parmesan cheese, mustard, salt and nutmeg. Whisk until well blended. Coarsely chop artichokes. Drain spinach and squeeze dry. Add artichokes and spinach to egg mixture. Stir to blend. Divide mixture evenly into 6 buttered ramekins or large baking dish. Sprinkle with remaining Monterey Jack cheese. Bake for 25 to 30 minutes at 350 degrees. Yield: 6 servings

## Adagio Inn Appetizer

Dried apricots topped with goat cheese and glazed walnuts, drizzled with lavender honey.

### Fresh Crostini

❖ *Suggested wine pairing - Sparkling Wine*

Fresh tomatoes, finely chopped
Fresh mozzarella cheese, finely chopped
Fresh basil, finely sliced
Balsamic vinegar for sprinkling

In mixing bowl combine all ingredients and mix well. Serve with Crostini.

Photo courtesy of Wine Country Inn

## Wine Country Inn

On the web page for the Wine country Inn it states "Ned and Marge Smith decided to build a new 'old' Inn filled with antiques, handmade stitcheries and quilts". This description lead me to believe I was going to visit a quaint cottage type inn. To my surprise I found a large modern lodging complex.

Marge and Ned had visited bed and breakfasts in New England and knew exactly what they wanted in their inn. They found local artists and included their work in the inn. To assure a comfortable feeling in the rooms they added fireplaces and balconies with great views.

The main building was opened in 1975 with 24 guest rooms. It is a large building made of dark wood and stonework. Doug Smith, a son of Ned and Marge Smith, is a local builder and constructed this beautiful building. Another son, Jim did the stonework. He is now the Innkeeper. A third son is in charge of the 6 acres of vineyard that is part of their property. I learned the vineyard produces about 400 cases of Cabernet wine a year. It is receiving recognition from the wine world as an excellent "cult wine".

In 1982 The Brandy Barn was completed with six guest rooms. Later the Hastings House with four guest rooms was added. The five cottages on the property were the latest addition to meet the need for more space for guests.

Marge wanted an "old" country feeling in the rooms. She and her daughter Kate and grandmother Nummy made quilts and other hand stitched fabrics for decorations. Marge sought out and purchased antique furniture at auctions, antique shows and estate sales. I noted the round table and chairs in the dining room area were antique oak, each with a slightly different style. The set of four chairs at each table were different yet blended well in the setting.

The open dining area is also used for wine tasting. The guests not only sample the Wine Country Inn's product but other wineries often come to the Inn and present their wines to the guests at the afternoon refreshment event.

## Zucchini Bread

❖ *Zucchini Bread is done when wooden pick inserted in center comes out clean.*

2 eggs
1 cup sugar
1/2 cup vegetable oil
1 cup fresh zucchini, shredded with skin
1 teaspoon vanilla
1 1/2 cups all-purpose flour
1/2 teaspoon baking soda
1/2 teaspoon salt
1/8 teaspoon baking powder
1 1/2 teaspoons cinnamon
1/2 teaspoon nutmeg
1/2 teaspoon ginger

Preheat oven to 325 degrees. In large bowl beat eggs and sugar until foamy. Add oil, zucchini and vanilla. Stir to blend. Combine flour, baking soda, salt, baking powder and spices. Add dry ingredients to zucchini mixture. Mix well. Pour into greased and floured loaf pan (9 x 5 inch). Bake for one hour at 325 degrees until a wooden pick inserted in the center comes out clean.
Yield: 1 loaf

## Baked Apples

❖ *Serve apples with some of the pan juices.*

❖ *Apples can be baked at 150 degrees for 60 to 90 minutes if desired.*

❖ *Apples can be refrigerated after baking and heated in a microwave just before serving.*

6 Roma Beauty apples
3 pats butter (about 1 teaspoon each)
6 tablespoons brown sugar
1 teaspoon cinnamon
1/2 teaspoon ground cloves
1/3 cup walnuts, chopped
Apple juice as needed

Preheat oven to 325 degrees. Core each apple and slice very top off. Puncture bottom with fork several times. Place apples in baking dish. Sprinkle each apple with cinnamon and cloves. Stuff apples with 1/2 pat butter, 1 tablespoon brown sugar and walnuts. Pour 3/4 inch of apple juice in bottom of baking dish. Bake for 30 minutes at 325 degrees.
Yield: 6 servings

## Mexican Wedding Cakes

1 cup butter
3/4 cup powdered sugar
1 teaspoon vanilla
2 cups all-purpose flour, sifted
1 cup pecans, chopped

Preheat oven to 325 degrees. In mixing bowl beat butter until fluffy. Add sugar, flour and vanilla. Mix well. Blend in pecans. Roll dough into 1-inch balls. Place on greased cookie sheet. Bake for 25 minutes at 325 degrees. Remove from oven and sprinkle with powdered sugar.
Yield: 4 dozen

## Carrot Coconut Muffins

1 cup all-purpose flour
1 1/4 teaspoons baking powder
3/4 teaspoon baking soda
1 teaspoon cinnamon
1/4 teaspoon nutmeg
1/4 teaspoon salt
2 eggs
1 cup brown sugar
1/3 cup vegetable oil
2 tablespoons maple syrup
1/4 cup golden raisins
1/4 cup flaked coconut
1/2 cup canned crushed pineapple, well drained

Preheat oven to 350 degrees. In large mixing bowl combine flour, baking powder, baking soda, cinnamon, nutmeg and salt. In a separate bowl beat eggs until foamy. Add brown sugar, oil and syrup. Add egg mixture to dry ingredients. Mix well. Pour into greased and floured muffin cups. Bake for 30 minutes at 350 degrees, until a wooden pick inserted in center comes out clean.
Yield: 8 muffins

## Denver Casserole

2 large cloves garlic, minced
1 red bell pepper, diced
1 green bell pepper, diced
1/4 cup onion, diced
1 tablespoon vegetable oil
1 teaspoon fresh parsley, chopped
1 teaspoon fresh basil, chopped
6 eggs
1/2 cup sour cream
Salt and pepper to taste
3 slices Sourdough bread, cubed, no crust
1 cup cooked ham, cubed
1 cup fresh tomato, chopped
1 cup cheddar cheese, shredded

❖ *Vegetables can be prepared the day before and refrigerated over night.*

❖ *Suggested wine pairing - Pinot Grigio*

Preheat oven to 350 degrees. In skillet sauté garlic, peppers and onion in vegetable oil. Add parsley and basil. In separate bowl beat eggs with sour cream, salt and pepper. Add remaining ingredients and mix well to blend. Pour into greased 9-inch square baking dish (2 quart baking dish). Bake for 30 to 40 minutes at 350 degrees, until eggs are set. Let stand 10 minutes before serving.
Yield: 4 to 6 servings

## Ginger Pear Bread

3/4 cup sugar
2 eggs
1/3 cup vegetable oil
1 can (16 ounces) pears in own juice
1 teaspoon ground ginger
2 cups all-purpose flour
3/4 tablespoon baking powder
1/2 teaspoon salt

Preheat oven to 325 degrees. In mixing bowl combine sugar and eggs. Drain and chop pears. Add oil and pears. In separate bowl mix dry ingredients. Add egg pear mixture to dry ingredients. Stir to blend. Pour batter into greased or sprayed loaf pan. Bake for 50 minutes at 325 degrees.
Yield: 1 loaf

❖ *Cover with foil when top of bread is golden to prevent burning.*

## Poppy Seed Cake

3/4 cup sugar
1/2 cup vegetable oil
1 large egg
1 cup all-purpose flour
1/3 teaspoon vanilla
1/8 teaspoon salt
1/2 teaspoon baking soda
1/2 cup (4 ounces) evaporated milk
2 tablespoons poppy seeds

❖ *Poppy Seed Cake is done when wooden pick inserted in center comes out clean.*

Preheat oven to 350 degrees. In large bowl combine sugar, oil, egg and vanilla. Add all remaining ingredients. Mix well. Pour into well greased loaf pan. Bake for 1 hour 10 minutes at 350 degrees.
Yield: 1 loaf

## Whole Wheat Banana Bread

1/2 cup butter, melted
1 cup sugar
2 eggs, slightly beaten
3 medium size ripe bananas, mashed (1 cup)
1 cup all-purpose flour, sift before measuring
1 teaspoon baking soda
1/2 teaspoon salt
1 cup whole wheat flour
1/3 cup hot water
1/2 cup walnuts, chopped

❖ *Whole wheat flour enriches the flavor of this moist banana bread.*

❖ *Banana bread has a light cake-like texture.*

Preheat oven to 325 degrees. In mixing bowl blend melted butter and sugar. Mix in eggs and mashed bananas. Blend until smooth. Sift flour, baking soda and salt together. Stir in whole wheat flour. Add dry ingredients alternately with hot water to banana mixture. Add nuts, stir. Pour into greased 9 x 5 inch loaf pan. Bake for 1 hour and 10 minutes at 325 degrees.
Yield: 1 loaf

## Death by Cheese

6 eggs
1/2 cup all-purpose flour
1 teaspoon baking powder
1/8 teaspoon salt
1 cup milk
1 cup (8 ounces) cottage cheese
4 ounces cream cheese, cubed
2 cups Monterey Jack cheese, cut into cubes
2 tablespoons butter

❖ *The cream cheese and Monterey Jack cheese can be cubed the day before preparation of Death by Cheese, if desired.*

Preheat oven to 325 degrees. In a large bowl beat eggs. Add flour, baking powder, salt and milk. Whisk with wire whip until smooth. Beat in cottage cheese. Add cubed cheeses and stir so cream cheese cubes do not stick together. Pour into buttered baking dish. Dot top with butter. Bake for 45 minutes at 325 degrees, until puffed and golden brown. Allow to cool for 10 minutes. Cut into 8 equal squares.
Yield: 4 servings

❖ *If storing cubed cheese place in zip-lock bag to refrigerate.*

❖ *Suggested wine pairing - Extra Dry Champagne*

## Dilly Dip

1 cup sour cream
1 cup mayonnaise
1 tablespoon dill weed
1 tablespoon dried parsley
1 tablespoon green onion, chopped
Dash of ground pepper

In medium size bowl mix together all ingredients. Refrigerate until serving.
Yield: 2 cups

## Hot Artichoke Dip

❖ *For a "screaming" hot dip add chopped jalapenos.*

❖ *Serve with sourdough bread or crackers.*

1 cup mayonnaise
1 cup parmesan cheese, grated
1 cup cheddar cheese, grated
1 small can (4 ounces) green chilies, diced
1 can (16 ounces) artichokes, chopped
Ground pepper to taste

Preheat oven to 350 degrees. In mixing bowl mix all ingredients. Pour into baking dish. Bake for 25 minutes at 350 degrees.
Yield: 6 cups

## Italian White Bean and Pesto Dip

1/3 cup mayonnaise
1 can (16 ounces) garbanzo beans, drained
1 1/2 tablespoons lemon juice
1/4 teaspoon salt
1 1/2 heaping tablespoons pesto

In food processor blend all ingredients until smooth. Mix with spoon twice during blending. Blend for 1 to 2 minutes. Cover and chill for 2 hours before serving.
Yield: 2 1/2 cups

❖ *Dip should not be runny.*

❖ *Dip will keep covered in refrigerator for 2 weeks.*

## Roasted Red Bell Pepper Dip

1 cup mayonnaise
1/2 cup sour cream
1/2 jar (6 ounces) roasted red peppers
1 teaspoon dried basil
1/2 teaspoon garlic, minced

In food processor blend all ingredients until smooth. Do not over blend. Refrigerate for 1 hour before serving.
Yield: 2 cups

❖ *Use less garlic for a milder dip.*

❖ *Pat red peppers with paper towel to remove excess moisture.*

❖ *If mixture is over beaten it becomes runny.*

## Spinach Dip

1 box (10 ounces) frozen spinach, chopped
2 cups sour cream
1 cup mayonnaise
1/2 cup red onion, chopped
1 can (7 ounces) water chestnuts, chopped
1/2 teaspoon black pepper
1 teaspoon salt

❖ *Suggested wine pairings -*
*Viognier*
*Chardonnay*

Thaw spinach and squeeze out liquid. Drain water chestnuts. Combine all ingredients. Refrigerate for 1 hour before serving.
Yield: 4 cups

## Must Go Rolls

❖ *Pillsbury refrigerated croissant*
*dough is suggested.*

❖ *Stone ground mustard can be*
*used in place of spicy mustard.*

4 sausages, squeezed out of casing
25 to 30 mushrooms, sliced
1 red onion, diced
1/4 cup Port wine
1/2 cup sour cream
2 tablespoons spicy prepared mustard
2 tubes croissant dough

Preheat oven to 375 degrees. In skillet cook sausage, mushrooms, onion and Port wine, until most of the liquid is gone. Add sour cream and mustard. Stir to blend. Open tubes of dough. Unroll each roll of dough onto cookie sheet. Make a line of filling down middle of each length. Wrap dough over filling and pinch ends. Bake for 11 minutes at 375 degrees, until golden brown. Cut into bite size pieces.
Yield: 12 to 24 rolls

## Maison Fleurie

The Magnolia Hotel in Yountville was built by Pierre Gullium in 1873. The two and one half story rectangular building of native stone is one of only three stone buildings in Yountville. It stands not far from the first train depot and near the early Groezinger Wine Cellars.

The Hotel originally included a saloon, one of a dozen or more in 19th century Yountville. Being located close to the depot and Groezinger Winery assured a steady clientele. The hotel also prospered. It was rumored that some "ladies of ill repute" may have also visited the hotel.

Pierre had no children so when he died he willed his property, including the Magnolia Hotel to John Lande, Peter Lande, Judge Shefflitte and Father Carmedy. The Monsignor advised Father Carmedy to sell his share. John Lande purchased Father Carmedy's holdings. He later bought out the other share holders.

John ran the hotel and restaurant until the late 1940's. By 1950 the hotel was being used as a community center. The 4-H Club and the Boy Scouts held their meetings in the hotel. A local ladies sewing club would gather once a week in what was once the hotel dinning room.

In the 1960's the building was abandoned and remained empty until 1969 when Nancy and Ray Monte purchased the property for fifty thousand dollars. The Monte's had sold their cattle ranch because the land was becoming more valuable for raising grapes.

The inside of the Magnolia Hotel was completely gutted. The only access to the second floor was by a ladder. The Monte's spent two years and three months restoring the building to its original glory. One of the major jobs was removing about 2 feet of dirt from the cellar. The job was made less tedious for Ray and the children because of the treasures found in the dirt. They found Guillium tokens, spring water bottles from 1915 and other memorabilia from the early years of the hotel.

When completed they covered the cement floor with French tile and created an intimate dining room to seat 22 people for dinner. The upstairs dining room also seated 24 guests. Four bedrooms each with private bath were built on the second floor. The two bedrooms on the third level were the children's bedrooms, however, the children were willing to rent their quarters to guests as long as they could share in the income. The rooms rented for $30.00 a night but later increased to $50.00 for a double room.

In 1977 Bruce and Bonnie Locken made an offer to buy the Magnolia Hotel as a bed and breakfast. Ray was fifty five years old and liked the idea of retiring. They sold the inn and bought a sailboat that they lived on for eleven years.

After Bruce Locken died Bonnie continued to run the bed and breakfast. In 1995 she sold the inn to the Post family. The new owners changed most of the furniture, the furnishings and decorations. They changed the name to Maison Fleurie. It now operates as a bed and breakfast.

## Cobblestone Hobo Breakfast

5 large red potatoes
1 large onion, chopped
1 tablespoon butter
1 tablespoon vegetable oil
Paprika for browning agent
Salt and pepper to taste
3 tablespoons fresh parsley, chopped

❖ *Stir potatoes as little as possible while frying.*

Boil potatoes in salted water until just tender. Drain, cool and cut into cubes. Sauté onion until tender. In separate pan melt butter with oil. Add potatoes, paprika, salt and pepper. Fry until brown and crisp. Stir in parsley and onions.

❖ *Suggested wine pairings -
    Beaujolais
    Pinot Noir*

### Cream Sauce
1/4 cup butter
1/4 cup all-purpose flour
1 cup half and half cream
1 tablespoon lemon juice
1/4 cup cooked bacon, crumbled
Salt and pepper to taste

In small sauce pan melt butter. Add flour and cook over medium heat stirring constantly for 2 to 3 minutes. Add cream, cook until thickened stirring to prevent lumps. Add lemon juice and bacon bits.
Yield: 2 cups

### Poached eggs
8 eggs
1 tablespoon white vinegar
1 cup cheddar cheese, shredded

Fill sauté pan half full of unsalted water. Add vinegar. Crack eggs gently into boiling water. Poach about 3 minutes. Remove carefully with slotted spoon. Place a layer of potatoes in quiche pan. Reheat in oven. Add layer cheddar cheese. Return to oven to melt. Gently place poached egg on top of hot mixture. Top with dollops of cream sauce. Garnish with parsley.
Yield: 8 servings

## Lemon Yogurt Cake

1 cup sweet butter
3 cups sugar
5 eggs
1 teaspoon vanilla
2 3/4 cups all-purpose flour
1/2 teaspoon salt
1/2 teaspoon baking soda
1 cup plain yogurt
1/4 cup lemon juice
Zest of one lemon

Preheat oven to 350 degrees. In mixing bowl cream butter and sugar. Add eggs one at a time. Add vanilla. Combine dry ingredients and butter mixture, alternating with yogurt, lemon juice and zest. Pour batter into greased and floured bundt pan. Bake for 45 to 50 minutes at 350 degrees. Remove from bundt pan and glaze top of warm cake.
Yield: 10-inch Bundt cake

❖ *Glaze can be prepared the day ahead of serving. Heat glaze before pouring over the warm cake.*

## Lemon Glaze
1/2 cup lemon juice
1/2 cup sugar
1/4 cup water

In sauce pan combine all ingredients and cook for 10 to 15 minutes, until it becomes a syrup. Pour over warm cake.
Yield: 1 cup

## Cheddar Cheese Popovers

1 cup all-purpose flour
4 eggs, beaten
1/8 teaspoon salt
1/8 teaspoon pepper
1 1/2 cups half and half cream
4 tablespoons butter, melted
1 cup cheddar cheese, grated
1/4 cup fresh chives, chopped

❖ *If batter is too thin add
   more flour.*

❖ *Recipe can be cut into half for a
   smaller amount.*

❖ *Greased popover cups can be
   used for baking popovers.
   Bake 20 minutes.*

Preheat oven to 400 degrees. In mixing bowl combine flour, eggs, salt and pepper. Add cream and butter. Stir in cheese and chives. Drop onto greased cookie sheet. Bake 15 minutes at 400 degrees. Yield: 12 popovers

## Mexican Quiche

6 eggs
1/4 cup all-purpose flour
1 teaspoon baking soda
1 can (7 ounces) green chilies, chopped
2 cups cottage cheese
2 cups cheddar cheese, grated
1/2 cup half and half cream

❖ *Suggested wine pairing -
   Off-dry Reisling*

Preheat oven to 400 degrees. In mixing bowl combine eggs, flour and baking soda. Add chilies, cheeses and cream. Pour into quiche pan. Bake for 35 to 40 minutes at 400 degrees, until set. Yield: 8 servings

## Remington's Prawns Prosciutto

24 large prawns, peeled and deveined
24 fresh basil leaves
24 thin slices Prosciutto (1 inch by 4 inches)

Slice prawns lengthwise one inch up from tail. Wrap each with basil leaf and Prosciutto. Grill and serve with Beurre Blanc Sauce.
Yield: 8 servings

### Beurre Blanc Sauce
1 tablespoon shallots
1/8 teaspoon white pepper
1/2 cup dry white wine
1/4 cup flavored vinegar
1/4 cup heavy cream
1 1/4 cups butter, softened
Lemon juice to flavor

In sauce pan combine shallots, pepper, white wine and vinegar. Cook over medium heat. Reduce to about 2 tablespoons of liquid. Add cream. Simmer 5 minutes. Whisk in butter until smooth. Add lemon juice to flavor.
Yield: 8 servings

❖ *Skewer prawns to kabob sticks for easier grilling.*

❖ *This dish pairs well with Grilled Asparagus and Champagne Vinaigrette (see following pages).*

❖ *Suggested wine pairings -*
*Semillon*
*Buttery-style Chardonnay*

## Champignons Frits

1/2 pound mushrooms
1/2 cup all-purpose flour
2 eggs, beaten
1 cup bread crumbs
2 cups vegetable oil for frying
Salt to taste
Lemon wedge for garnish

Wash and quarter mushrooms. Place flour in one container, beaten eggs in another and bread crumbs in a third. Bread mushrooms by dipping them first in flour then egg then bread crumbs. Fry mushrooms in hot oil until golden brown. Remove mushrooms from oil using strainer, allowing excess oil to drip off. Salt lightly. Serve with tarter sauce and lemon wedge.
Yield: 4 servings

### Tartar Sauce

❖ *If sauce is too thick, add a little pickle juice to thin.*

❖ *Store tartar sauce covered in refrigerator.*

1/2 cup mayonnaise
1 dill pickle, chopped
2 tablespoons chives, chopped
1/3 cup green onions, chopped
Pickle juice, if needed

In mixing bowl combine all ingredients. Stir to blend.
Yield: 1 cup

## Grilled Asparagus

12 medium size fresh asparagus spears
1/2 teaspoons olive oil
Salt and pepper to taste
3 tablespoons (1 1/2 ounces) Asiago cheese, grated

Preheat oven to 425 degrees. Blanch asparagus in boiling water for 5 seconds. Drain. Baste with 1/2 teaspoon olive oil. Add salt and pepper to taste. Grill or broil asparagus until gently browned. Place on baking tray. Generously top with Asiago cheese. Bake for approximately 7 minutes at 425 degrees, until cheese is golden brown. Carefully remove the asparagus from the tray and place on serving platter. Top with champagne vinaigrette.
Yield: 4 servings

❖ *Garnish the asparagus with parsley and fresh cracked black pepper.*

❖ *The amount of vinegar can be increased to add more flavor.*

### Champagne Vinaigrette
1 1/2 tablespoons olive oil
1 tablespoon walnut oil
1/4 teaspoon champagne vinegar
1/4 teaspoon salt
1/8 teaspoon pepper

Place all ingredients in blender. Blend until smooth. Refrigerate.
Yield: 2 1/2 tablespoons

## Raspberry Coffee Cake

3 ounces cream cheese, softened
1/4 cup sweet butter, softened
2 cups baking mix (Bisquick)
1/3 cup milk
1/2 cup raspberry jam

Preheat oven to 425 degrees. In large bowl cut the cream cheese and butter into baking mix until crumbly. Add milk and knead on lightly floured surface. Place dough on wax paper. Roll into an 8 x 12 inch rectangle. Transfer onto greased baking sheet. Remove wax paper. Spread jam down center of dough. Make 2 1/2 inch cuts at 1 inch intervals on the long side of the rectangle. Fold the strips over the filling, sealing the ends. Bake for 12 to 15 minutes at 425 degrees. Drizzle icing over top.
Yield: 8 to 10 servings

### Coffee Cake Icing
1 cup powdered sugar
1 1/2 tablespoons milk
1/4 teaspoon vanilla

In small mixing bowl combine all ingredients Stir until smooth. Drizzle over coffee cake.

## Chocolate Meringue Cookies

❖ *Cool chocolate completely before adding stiff egg white mixture or egg whites will break down.*

❖ *Chopped walnuts, pecans or toasted almonds can be used as desired in this recipe.*

3 large egg whites
3/4 cup sugar
3/4 cup (6 ounces) bittersweet chocolate
1 1/2 teaspoons vanilla
1/2 cup nuts, chopped

Preheat oven to 350 degrees. Melt chocolate over warm water. Cool and set aside. In mixing bowl beat egg whites to soft peaks. Continue beating while gradually adding sugar. Beat until stiff and glossy. Fold in melted chocolate, vanilla and nuts. Drop by teaspoonfuls onto parchment lined cookie sheet. Bake for 10 to 20 minutes at 350 degrees. Cool cookies completely on trays before removing
Yield: 2 dozen cookies

## *Lavender*

The house that is now the Lavender Bed and Breakfast was once a frame farmhouse located on Captain John Grigsby's ranch. The ranch was only a few miles southeast of Yountville. Captain Grigsby was an active supporter of the Bear Flag Rebellion. The Rebellion was a protest by the settlers and frontiersman against the rules and regulations imposed by the Mexican Government. The ranch was the center for the Napa County men to meet with Captain John C. Fremont, of the U. S. Army and a leader of the Rebellion.

The farmhouse was bought by John Webber in 1890 and moved to the town of Yountville. The street where the house was placed is Webber Street, named after John Webber who was a County Supervisor from the district in the early 1900's. Later his son Samuel became a County Supervisor.

The farmhouse with clapboard siding was originally a simple gable roofed house in the Greek revival style. Soon after the move to Yountville the second story extension was added and additions made on the side of the house. A one story porch that wraps around the front and side supported with plain square columns was attached. The double-hung windows with plain moldings were installed. A carriage house was built for the horses and buggies and later housed automobiles.

The Webber family lived in the house until 1929.

Since that time there have been several owners. In 1970 Loren Holte was the owner of the "Webber Place" as it was known. It was converted into a bed and breakfast and not surprising was called the Webber Place.

Diane Barthelium had lived in Berkeley, California for 25 years before coming to Yountville. As an artist she felt living in a small town in the wine country would be a great environment for her paintings. In 1983 Diane purchased the Webber Place from the Holte's. At that time the Inn had eight guest rooms. With a change in Yountville's regulations the number of rooms was reduced to four. After many years of negotiations she finally received a permit to have eight rooms in her bed and breakfast.

By 1997 Diane was ready for a change and a rest. She sold the Inn to Roger and Sally Post, owners of the Four Sisters Inns. The Posts had four daughters and honored them by naming the company for the four girls. Today they are running the company.

The new owners made renovations using the architectural plans that Diane had drawn up after receiving the permit for more rooms. Other changes were made to modernize the home. The name of the Inn became Lavender. According to Diane, to add authenticity to the name they planted lavender in the yard.

## Bircher Muesli

1/2 cup raisins
1/2 cup old fashioned oatmeal
1 1/2 cups quick cooking oatmeal
1/3 cup brown sugar
1/4 to 1/2 teaspoon cinnamon
2 cups milk or half and half cream
Fresh fruit

In large bowl mix all ingredients, except fresh fruit. Let set overnight in refrigerator. Add fresh fruit when ready to serve.
Yield: 4 cups

❖ *Bircher Muesli was originally made at the Swiss clinic run by Dr. Bircher-Benner at the turn of the century (1900). This is a variation of his classic breakfast dish.*

❖ *The chef adds their touch to the recipe. Some additions are walnuts, apples, banana, fresh berries or coconut.*

❖ *Muesli keeps in the refrigerator for 4 to 5 days.*

## Chile Relleno Strata

1 can (12 ounces) whole green chilies
2 cups Monterey Jack cheese, grated
12 eggs, beaten
1/2 cup half and half cream
1/2 cup milk
1 teaspoon salt
Dash hot sauce (Tabasco)

Preheat oven to 350 degrees. In a well-greased quiche pan layer half of the chilies on the bottom so the ends point to the center of the pan. Cover with cheese and remaining chilies. Mix eggs, cream, milk, salt and hot sauce together. Pour over chilies. Bake for 60 minutes at 350 degrees until strata is set.
Yield: 8 servings

## Sour Cream Orange Cake

1 1/2 cups sweet butter, softened
1 3/4 cups sugar
4 large eggs, room temperature
1/2 teaspoon lemon zest
1/2 teaspoon orange zest
1/2 teaspoon vanilla
3 cups all-purpose flour
3 teaspoons baking powder
1 teaspoon baking soda
1/2 teaspoon salt
1 1/2 cups sour cream

Preheat oven to 350 degrees. In large mixing bowl cream butter and sugar. Add eggs, one at a time beating after each addition. Stir in lemon, orange zest and vanilla. Set aside. In separate bowl sift together flour, baking powder, baking soda and salt. Add dry ingredients to butter mixture, alternately with sour cream. Stir well after each addition, but do not over beat. Pour into greased and floured bundt pan. Bake for 50 to 60 minutes at 350 degrees until wooden pick inserted in center comes out clean. Cool before removing from bundt pan. Invert onto plate and cover with glaze.
Yield: 12 servings

❖ *This beautiful bundt cake is a welcome birthday cake.*

❖ *Cake glaze can be prepared the day before serving. Simply reheat glaze before pouring onto the cake.*

### Cake Glaze
1/2 cup orange juice
2 tablespoons sugar
3 tablespoons orange liqueur
1 tablespoon lemon juice

In sauce pan combine all ingredients. Bring to boil. Cook over medium heat for 2 to 3 minutes. Pour warm glaze over cooled cake. Let stand for 10 or more minutes before serving.
Yield: 1 cup

# Crab and Cheese Soufflé Toasts

❖ *Garnish serving dish with fresh dill.*

❖ *The Crab and Cheese Soufflé Toasts make great tasting appetizers.*

❖ *Suggested wine pairing - Gewürztraminer*

## Soufflé
2 egg whites
1/2 cup mayonnaise
1/2 cup cheddar cheese, grated
1/4 cup green onions, chopped
1 tablespoon fresh parsley, chopped
1 tablespoon fresh dill, chopped
Salt and white pepper to taste
Cayenne pepper to taste

Beat egg whites until stiff. In separate bowl mix mayonnaise, cheese, onions, parsley, dill, salt, white pepper and cayenne pepper. Fold mixture into beaten egg whites.

## Toast Rounds
1 loaf French bread, cut 1/2 inch thick slices
1 cup butter, softened
2 cloves garlic, minced
1/4 cup parmesan cheese, grated
1/2 cup (4 ounces) crab meat

Blend butter and garlic. Spread on bread rounds. Sprinkle with parmesan cheese. Lightly toast under broiler. Place heaping tablespoon of crab meat on each toast. Top with 1 tablespoon soufflé mixture. Place toast rounds under broiler for 2 to 3 minutes until cheese is lightly browned.
Yield: 6 servings

## Buttermilk Oatmeal Biscuits

1/2 cup rolled oats oatmeal
1 3/4 cups all-purpose flour
1/2 teaspoon salt
1 teaspoon baking powder
1/2 teaspoon baking soda
4 tablespoons sweet butter, chilled
3/4 cup buttermilk

Preheat oven to 425 degrees. In mixing bowl combine oats, flour, salt, baking powder and baking soda. Cut butter into pieces and add to the flour mixture. Using your fingers or pastry cutter cut the butter into the flour mixture until coarse texture. Add buttermilk. Stir with fork until dough partially holds together. Place dough on lightly floured surface. Knead about 10 times. Pat or roll into 1/2 inch thickness. Cut into 2 inch rounds. Place 1 inch apart on greased baking sheet. Bake for 12 to 15 minutes at 425 degrees.
Yield: 12 biscuits

## Raspberry Butter
1/2 cup sweet butter
2 cups fresh raspberries
2/3 cup sugar

In small sauce pan melt butter. Stir in raspberries and sugar. Stir until sugar is completely dissolved.
Yield: 3 cups

❖ *Add additional sugar if necessary for sweetness.*

❖ *Store in airtight container in refrigerator.*

❖ *Raspberry butter will keep in the refrigerator for two weeks.*

# Artichoke Pesto Puffs

**Pesto**
2 bunches basil, chopped
1/4 cup olive oil
1/4 cup parmesan cheese
1/2 cup pine nuts
Salt and pepper to taste

❖ *Pesto can be stored in the refrigerator for 3 days.*

Place all ingredients in food processor. Blend well.

❖ *Finely chop sun-dried tomatoes.*

❖ *Unused frozen puff pastry sheets can be refrozen if wrapped in plastic and foil.*

❖ *Suggested wine pairing - Sauvignon Blanc*

**Puffs**
5 cups artichokes, chopped
1/4 cup pesto
3 tablespoons olive oil
1/4 cup white wine
2 tablespoons sun-dried tomatoes, chopped
2 tablespoons parsley, chopped
1 cup feta cheese, crumbled
1/2 cup parmesan cheese, grated
2 sheets puff pastry
Balsamic vinegar for dipping

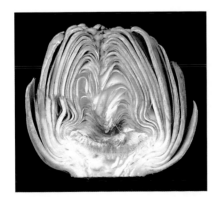

Preheat oven to 425 degrees. Finely chop artichokes. Sauté over medium heat. Add pesto, sun-dried tomatoes and 2 tablespoon olive oil. Stir for several minutes to blend. Add wine and cook for 3 to 5 minutes. Remove from heat. Add parsley and feta cheese. Mix well. Roll one pastry sheet into 8 x 12 inch rectangle. Cut into 4-inch squares. Fill each square with 2 teaspoons of artichoke mixture. Fold pastry side over mixture to form a pocket. Seal edges securely by pinching together. Brush with remaining olive oil. Cover with plastic. Repeat with second puff pastry sheet. Refrigerate for 15 minutes. Sprinkle top with parmesan cheese. Bake for 20 to 25 minutes at 425 degrees, until golden brown. Yield: 8 servings

## Potato Pancakes

2 eggs, beaten
2 tablespoons all-purpose flour
1/4 teaspoon baking powder
1 teaspoon salt
1/8 teaspoon black pepper
1/4 cup fresh chives, chopped
1 1/2 cups potatoes, shredded
Oil for frying

In mixing bowl combine eggs, flour, baking powder, salt, pepper and chives. Stir to blend. Add potatoes and stir to blend. Drop by large spoonfuls onto buttered hot skillet. Fry on both sides until golden brown. Yield: 10 pancakes

## Tomato Roquefort Tart Provencal

1 9-inch pie crust, baked
4 tablespoons olive oil
1 clove garlic, sliced
1 clove shallot, sliced
4 fresh tomatoes, sliced
3 eggs
2 1/2 cups heavy cream
2 tablespoons fresh basil, chopped
2 tablespoons fresh parsley, chopped
5 ounces Roquefort cheese, crumbled
1/4 pound cooked ham, diced
Paprika, salt and pepper to taste

❖ *Allow tart to rest for 5 minutes before slicing.*

❖ *The Tomato Roquefort Tart is very attractive. Bring the whole tart to the table so all can see it before slicing.*

❖ *Garnish with greens, kale, lettuce or watercress.*

Preheat oven to 375 degrees. In skillet heat oil and sauté garlic and shallots. Whisk eggs and cream together. Add 1 tablespoon basil and 1 tablespoon parsley, cheese and ham. Season with paprika, salt and pepper. Arrange shallot mixture and 2 sliced tomatoes on the pie crust. Pour egg mixture over tomatoes in crust. Bake for 25 minutes at 375 degrees. Remove from oven. Arrange remaining tomatoes, basil and parsley on top of tart. Return to oven and bake for 5 additional minutes. Place under broiler for 3 minutes. Yield: 8 servings

## Coffee Pecan Muffins

**Batter**
1/2 cup sweet butter, melted
2 cups brown sugar
3/4 cup milk
1 teaspoon vanilla
1 egg
2 tablespoons brewed instant coffee
1 3/4 cups all-purpose flour
1 tablespoon baking powder
1/4 teaspoon salt
1/2 cup pecans, coarsely chopped

❖ *Brew instant coffee according to directions.*

❖ *The subtle coffee flavor makes these muffins very popular.*

Preheat oven to 350 degrees. In mixing bowl cream butter and sugar. Add milk, vanilla, egg and coffee. Mix well. In separate bowl combine flour, baking powder, salt and chopped pecans. Add the wet ingredients to dry ingredients. Stir until just mixed. Fill greased muffin cups 3/4 full. Sprinkle sugar pecan topping on each muffin. Bake for 15 to 20 minutes at 350 degrees.
Yield: 10 muffins

**Sugar Pecan Topping**
1 tablespoon sugar
2 tablespoons pecans, finely chopped

In small mixing bowl combine ingredients. Mix to coat pecans with sugar.
Yield: 3 tablespoons

# *Blackbird Inn*

Scott Warner knows more about the Blackbird Inn than anyone. Although the house was built in 1905 he rebuilt it in 2000. The first owner of the home was the first car dealer in Napa and wanted a home on what was known as millionaire road. The Arts and Crafts style building resembled a brown box. In 1970 an insurance company purchased the building and converted it into offices. When they outgrew the space the building was put on the market. It was for sale for 6 months before Scott purchased it.

Scott gutted the entire building. He had decided to restore the house to the Arts and Craft style of the early 1900. His inspiration was the Gamble House of Pasadena. He studied the books and records to find the authentic style for the structure. The large front door with glass patterns was copied from the Green and Green design of the 1900's.

The woodwork, the stairs, the doors and door frames, and the built-in buffet are all of mahogany with ebony pegs, handles and accent points. The banister of the stairs are wider then most we see today. It is a rich soft reddish brown that is warm and invites you to touch it. The stairs were done by Steward Caskie.

The furniture is hand made with quarter sawn oak. Scott found the design for many of the pieces in books about the Arts and Crafts period. He used these as patterns for the tables, cabinets and even the picture frames. He told me the chairs were inspired by a chair he found in the dump. He brought this discarded chair home to his work shop and took it apart to use as the pattern of the dining area chairs that he proceeded to make. They sit next to small round tables with a lily pad pattern top. Scott found a Charles Stickley designed chair that was priced at $10,000. He studied the chair, made measurements and duplicated the chair.

Even the light fixtures were carefully designed. The multiple hanging lights all at a different level were made by a company in Berkeley using a picture found in a book showing lights of the period. Sue Johnson of Berkeley made wall and some free standing light shades of white mica. To incase the real leaves in the design she separated the mica into thin sheets and placed the leaves between the layers of mica.

Another unique feature of the home is the large stone fireplace in the main room. It must be nine feet long. Scott had four tons of granite rocks brought to the house for the fireplace and for the landscaping.

Scott has made the Blackbird Inn an excellent example of museum quality Arts and Crafts style.

## Clafoutis Limousin

❖ *Frozen whole pitted cherries can be substituted for the fresh cherries in this recipe.*

❖ *Clafoutis Limousin is a delicious dessert served with a dollop of whipped cream or a scoop of vanilla ice cream.*

❖ *A few drops of cherry liqueur to the whipped cream adds zing to the dessert.*

4 cups (1 1/2 pounds) fresh cherries
1 cup milk
3 eggs
1 egg yolk
1 1/2 teaspoons vanilla
1/3 cup sugar
1/2 cup all-purpose flour
1/8 teaspoon salt
1/2 teaspoon cinnamon
Powdered sugar

Preheat oven to 350 degrees. Stem and pit cherries. Place cherries and juice from pitting in shallow 2-quart buttered baking dish. Mix remaining ingredients, except for powdered sugar in blender or food processor. Blend until smooth. Pour mixture over cherries. Bake for 40 minutes at 350 degrees. Remove from oven and sprinkle with powdered sugar.
Yield: 8 servings

## Potato Kugel

❖ *This dish can be prepared a day before serving and refrigerated unbaked. Add hot oil just before baking.*

3 medium potatoes
2 eggs, beaten
1 medium onion, finely chopped
1/2 teaspoon salt
1/8 teaspoon pepper
2 tablespoons bread crumbs
2 tablespoons vegetable oil

Preheat oven to 350 degrees. Coarsely grate potatoes and squeeze out as much liquid as possible. Set aside. In a large bowl place beaten eggs, potatoes, onion, salt, pepper and bread crumbs. Place oil in 9-inch baking dish. Place in hot oven for 5 minutes. Pour hot oil over potatoes mixture. Stir to blend. Pour into hot baking dish. Bake for 1 hour at 350 degrees.
Yield: 4 servings

## Toasted Almond Cheesecake

**Crust**
1/2 cup sweet butter, melted
2 cups chocolate cookie crumbs
1 cup toasted almonds, finely ground

**Filling**
12 ounces chocolate chips, melted
1 teaspoon cocoa powder, unsweetened
1 teaspoon almond extract
4 packages (8 ounces each) cream cheese
2 cups sugar
4 eggs
2 cups sour cream

Preheat oven to 350 degrees. For the crust mix together melted butter, cookie crumbs and ground almonds. Press into bottom of springform pan. Chill. Melt chocolate chips over warm water. Add cocoa powder and almond extract. Set aside. In mixing bowl beat cream cheese until light and fluffy. Gradually add sugar. Add eggs one at a time, mixing well after each addition until batter is smooth. Add cooled chocolate and sour cream. Pour into crust and bake for 1 hour and 45 minutes at 350 degrees. Cool completely before refrigerating.
Yield: 12 servings

❖ *The crust can be made with crushed graham crackers, if desired.*

❖ *Refrigerate cake before serving.*

## Mustard Peppercorn Dip

1 1/4 cups mayonnaise
1/3 cup Dijon mustard
1 medium clove garlic, minced
1/2 bunch parsley
1 1/2 teaspoons whole green peppercorns

In a food processor blend mayonnaise, mustard and garlic until smooth. Garnish with parsley sprigs and whole green peppercorns.
Yield: 6 servings

❖ *Serve dip with fresh vegetables.*

## White Chocolate Chunk Macadamia Nut Cookies

1 cup sweet butter, softened
1 cup brown sugar, dark
3/4 cup sugar
1 tablespoon vanilla
2 eggs
3 cups all-purpose flour
1/4 teaspoon salt
3/4 teaspoon baking soda
1 cup macadamia nuts, chopped
3 cup white chocolate chunks

❖ *These cookies are best when very pale in color.*

❖ *If white chocolate chunks are not available the white chocolate chips can be used.*

Preheat oven to 350 degrees. In mixing bowl cream butter and sugars until light and fluffy. Beat in vanilla and eggs until well blended, about 4 minutes. Add flour, salt and baking soda, mix well. Stir in nuts and white chocolate. Drop by tablespoon on greased cookie sheet. Bake for 8 to 10 minutes at 350 degrees.
Yield: 3 dozen cookies

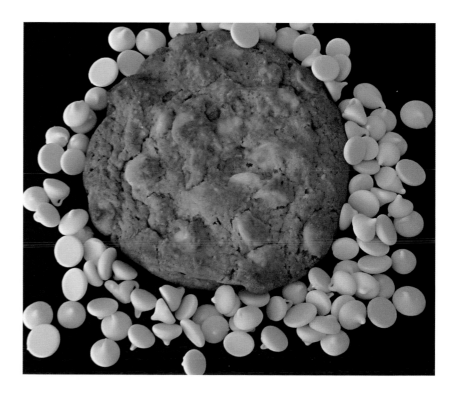

# Eggs Benedict

**White Sauce**
2 tablespoons butter
2 small leeks or 1 large leek, white and tender green parts only
1/3 cup butter
1/3 cup all-purpose flour
2 cups half and half cream
Salt and pepper to taste

**Filling**
6 eggs, poached
3 English muffins, lightly toasted
6 pieces Canadian bacon
3/4 cup cheddar cheese, grated
1/2 bunch parsley

Melt 2 tablespoons butter in skillet. Sauté leeks in butter until tender. Set aside. Place 1/2 cup butter in sauce pan, melt butter. Add flour and cook stirring constantly for 2 to 3 minutes. Add cream. Cook, stirring to desired consistency. Add salt and pepper to taste. Add leeks. Stir to blend. Arrange ham and poached egg on top of one half English muffin. Pour sauce over egg. Top with cheese. Garnish with parsley.
Yield: 6 servings

❖ *For more zing add a tablespoon of lemon juice to the sauce just before serving.*

❖ *This is a different sauce for Eggs Benedict and adds a new taste. Hollandaise is generally served with Eggs Benedict.*

❖ *If sauce is thick add more half and half.*

❖ *Suggested wine pairing -*
*Mimosa*
*Sparkling Wine*

## Mushroom Quiche

1 cup fresh mushrooms, sliced
1/4 cup onion, chopped
2 teaspoons olive oil
1 cup Swiss cheese, grated
1/2 cup parmesan cheese, grated
1/2 teaspoon dried thyme, crushed
1/2 teaspoon dried oregano, crushed
8 eggs
2 cups milk
1 cup heavy cream
Salt and pepper to taste

❖ *Let quiche set for 5 minutes before serving.*

❖ *Suggested wine pairing - Pinot Noir*

Preheat oven to 375 degrees. Sauté mushrooms and onions in oil. Spread half of cheese in bottom of greased quiche pan. Layer mushrooms and onions on top of cheese. Cover with remaining cheese. Sprinkle thyme and oregano over all. Whisk eggs, cream and salt and pepper together. Pour over top of quiche. Bake for 35 to 45 minutes at 375 degrees, until just set.
Yield: 6 to 8 servings

## Pineapple Coconut Muffins

❖ *The recipe for Pineapple Coconut muffins can be doubled for a larger number of muffins.*

1 cup all-purpose flour
1 1/2 teaspoons baking powder
2 tablespoons sugar
1/2 cup shredded coconut
1/3 teaspoon salt
1 egg
1/3 cup milk
2 tablespoons sweet butter, melted
1/4 cup crushed pineapple, drained

Preheat oven to 400 degrees. In mixing bowl combine flour, baking powder, sugar, coconut and salt. Add eggs, milk and butter. Stir in pineapple. Mix well. Spoon into greased muffin cups. Bake for 15 to 20 minutes at 400 degrees.
Yield: 6 muffins

## *Hennessey House*

The Hennessey House in Napa, California was built for Dr. Edwin Hennessey in 1889. It is a Queen Anne Victorian style home with Eastlake effect. The ceilings are high and the wood baseboards are about 15 inches tall. As of the time, the doors and windows are tall and narrow. The door frames have carved rosettes on each of the top corners. The original paneling and ornate moldings are still in place as is the hand painted stamped tin dining room ceiling that was probably installed in the 1930's. The front door has an insert of etched glass. As you enter into the foyer the open stairway* is on your right.

Dr. Hennessey was a prominent physician in Napa and built the home as a "state of the art" home at that time. He was known as a pioneer in x-ray technology in California in the early 1900's. He was also on the Board of Directors for the Veterans Home located near Yountville. At one time he was the mayor of the town of Napa.

In the early 1980's Robert Pitner bought the home and proceeded to renovate the nearly 100 year old house. He did save and preserve as many of the original features as possible. Changes were made in the front of the house, including the current porch and front doors. The original light fixtures are still in use. The stairwell and the entrance look much like they did in 1889. He proceeded to fill the home with European antiques. In 1985 he opened the home as a bed and breakfast.

In 1979 Alex and Jida Fret purchased the home and ran the bed and breakfast until 2004 when Lorri and Kevin Walsh became the owners. They were both executives in the high tech world. Kevin's job required that he travel and was away from his family a great deal. Lorri was working in chemical sales.

They had the idea of owning a bed and breakfast in the back of their minds. Lorri and Kevin decided to make a career change so they could spend more time with their 3 children. Lorri explained "one must enjoy what they are doing and running a bed and breakfast just fits us, it is part of who we are."

The Walsh's live in a house away from the bed and breakfast and have an innkeeper on site when they are not present. Lorri said she feels very fortunate to have a very good and dependable staff. The housekeeper has been at the Inn for 15 years and another staff person has been with the Inn for 6 years.

The Inn has a comfortable low key atmosphere. Lorri and Kevin remember the excess stress of the high tech world and hope the guests at the Inn can relax and "chill out".

## Chocolate Chip Banana Muffins

1 cup all-purpose flour
1/4 cup sugar
1/2 tablespoon baking powder
1/3 teaspoon cinnamon
1/4 teaspoon salt
1/2 cup milk
1/3 cup banana, mashed
2 tablespoons butter, melted
1 egg, slightly beaten
1/2 cup semi sweet chocolate chips
1/4 cup walnuts, chopped

❖ *Butterscotch chips can be substituted for chocolate chips.*

❖ *Nuts are optional and can be omitted if desired.*

Preheat oven to 400 degrees. In large bowl combine flour, sugar, baking powder, cinnamon and salt. Make a hole in the center. Add chocolate chips and nuts to coat. In small bowl combine milk, banana, butter and egg. Add to center of flour mixture. Stir until dry ingredients are just moistened. Spoon into greased muffin cups, filling each about 3/4 full. Bake for 18 to 20 minutes at 400 degrees. Cool 5 minutes in pan before removing.
Yield: 6 muffins

## Blue Cheese Spread with Walnuts

❖ *Serve with crackers, toast triangles or fresh vegetables.*

❖ *Ricotta cheese can be substituted for the cream cheese in this recipe.*

❖ *Suggested wine pairings -*
   *Zinfandel*
   *Syrah*

12 walnut halves, finely chopped
8 ounces cream cheese at room temperature
2 to 3 ounces blue cheese, room temperature
1 tablespoon cognac or other liqueur
Salt and pepper to taste
Chives, chopped

Chop walnuts in food processor. In bowl combine cheeses and mix with fork. Add liqueur, salt and pepper. Mix until smooth. Add walnuts and chives. Mix to blend.
Yield: approximately 1 cup

## Sun-Dried Tomato Muffins

1 cup all-purpose flour
1/2 tablespoon baking powder
1/4 teaspoon salt
1/8 teaspoon freshly ground black pepper
1/2 cup milk
1 egg
2 tablespoons olive oil
1/4 cup fresh grated parmesan cheese
1/4 cup sun-dried tomatoes in oil, chopped
1 teaspoon dried herbs of choice

❖ Recipe can be doubled for more muffins.

❖ Suggested herbs are oregano, thyme, rosemary and basil.

❖ Muffins are done when wooden pick inserted in center of the muffin comes out clean.

Preheat oven to 375 degrees. In a bowl combine dry ingredients. In medium bowl, whisk milk, egg and oil. Add cheese, sun-dried tomatoes and herb. Combine dry ingredients and egg mixture, stirring until just blended. Spoon into greased muffin cups. Bake for 20 minutes at 375 degrees. Cool for 5 minutes.
Yield: 6 muffins

## Cottage Cheese and Dill Muffins

1 cup all-purpose flour
1/2 tablespoon sugar
1 1/2 teaspoons baking powder
1/4 teaspoon baking soda
1/4 teaspoon salt
1 egg
1/2 cup milk
2 tablespoons butter, melted
1/2 tablespoon dill, fresh or dried, chopped
1/3 cup cottage cheese, small curd

❖ *The Cottage Cheese and Dill Muffins are delicious at breakfast and at lunch.*

Preheat oven to 375 degrees. In medium bowl combine dry ingredients. In separate bowl whisk together egg, milk, melted butter and dill, until well blended. Add cottage cheese. Add egg mixture to dry ingredients. Mix until just blended. Spoon into greased muffin cups, filling each cup 3/4 full. Bake for 18 to 20 minutes at 375 degrees.
Yield: approximately 8 muffins

## Artichoke Sun-Dried Tomato Strata

3 English muffins, split and quartered
1 tablespoon butter, melted
1/4 cup sun-dried tomatoes in oil, chopped
1/2 cup parmesan cheese, fresh, shredded
1 tablespoon green onions, finely chopped
1/2 cup artichoke hearts, chopped
6 eggs
2 cloves garlic, crushed
1/8 teaspoon nutmeg
1 can (12 ounces) evaporated milk

❖ *Cooked chopped ham can be substituted for the sun-dried tomatoes.*

Preheat oven to 375 degrees. Place muffins, crust side down, in sprayed baking dish. Drizzle with butter. Rinse sun-dried tomatoes and press with paper towel to remove oil. Layer tomatoes, cheese, onions and artichoke hearts over muffins. With electric mixer beat eggs until frothy. Add remaining ingredients. Mix. Pour egg mixture over muffins. Let stand for 30 minutes or overnight. Bake for 50 minutes at 375 degrees.
Yield: 6 servings

## Double Chocolate Chip Brownies

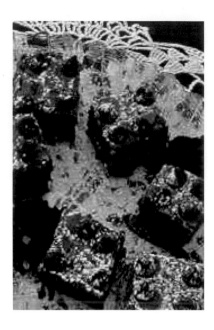

2 cups semi-sweet chocolate chips
1/2 cup butter, cut into pieces
3 eggs
1 1/4 cups all-purpose flour
1 cup sugar
1/4 teaspoon baking soda
1 teaspoon vanilla
1/2 cup nuts, chopped

Preheat oven to 350 degrees. In large heavy duty saucepan melt 1 cup chocolate chips and butter. Stir until smooth. Remove from heat. Stir in eggs, flour, sugar, baking soda and vanilla. Add remaining chips and nuts. Stir to blend. Spread into greased 11 x 7 inch baking pan. Bake for 30 minutes at 350 degrees. Cool on wire rack.
Yield: 2 dozen brownies

❖ *If doubling this recipe pour batter into 2 pans.*

❖ *If you double this recipe using one large pan the baking time increases to 45 minutes to 1 hour.*

❖ *Test for consistency with wooden prick inserted in center. If done, it will come out slightly sticky but almost clean.*

# Poppy Seed Orange Cake

3 cups all-purpose flour
1 1/2 teaspoons baking powder
3 eggs
1 1/2 cups vegetable oil
1 1/2 cups milk
2 cups sugar
1 1/2 tablespoons poppy seeds
1 1/2 teaspoons vanilla
1 1/2 teaspoons almond extract
1 1/2 teaspoons butter flavor extract

❖ *One teaspoon orange zest can be added to the cake batter.*

Preheat oven to 350 degrees. In mixing bowl stir by hand all ingredients. Mix until smooth. Grease or spray 3 half-loaf pans with non-stick cooking spray. Pour batter into pans. Bake for 1 hour at 350 degrees. While still hot make holes in cake using a tooth pick. Pour icing over loaves.
Yield: 3 loaves

## Cake Icing
1/4 cup orange juice
1/3 cup sugar
1/4 teaspoon vanilla
1/4 teaspoon almond extract
1/4 teaspoon butter flavor extract

In bowl mix all ingredients until sugar is dissolved. Spoon over warm cakes.

*Beazley House*

The Beazley house was build by Dr. Adolph Kahn in 1902 and was used as the physician's office and residence. The family lived in the home for eight years until the couple divorced. Dr. Kahn moved to San Francisco and continued his practice of medicine. Their grandson recently returned to the Beazley house and recalled the happy times at this house when the family was all together. They never lived together as a family after the divorce.

The house went on the market and was purchased by Bert and Mary Voohees in 1910. They lived in the home until 1963 when the widowed Mrs. Voohees died. They did not have children to inherit the home.

In 1963 the house became the Hanna Boys Center, a Sonoma based boy's home for troubled boys or those with special needs. They used the home for nearly 15 years. The next owner was a flamboyant socialite from San Francisco. Mrs. Joan Hitchcock loved parties and was even involved in local politics. The house took on a completely different atmosphere from the time it was a boy's home. Unfortunately, Joan's life style did not help her health and she died at 49 years of age.

When Jim and Carol Beazley purchased the home in 1981 they made the mortgage payments to Joan Hitchcock's children for the next 7 years. They had not operated a bed and breakfast before and were pleased to have the advice and encouragement from the owners of the Chalet Bernensis, Essie and Jack Doty.

The Beazley's spent some time renovating the home to make it a bed and breakfast. It was the first bed and breakfast in Napa, California. I was impressed with the beautiful stained glass in the entry door. The pattern in the door resembles the stained glass window in the stair landing.

Carol's background is nursing. She has carried her concern for good health into her menus. You will find low fat and low cholesterol recipes of some of the food she serves her guests.

## Chocolate Chip Cookies

1 1/2 cups (3 sticks) butter, softened
1 cup sugar
1 cup brown sugar, not packed
2 eggs
2 teaspoons baking soda
4 teaspoons real vanilla or 6 teaspoons of imitation vanilla
4 cups all-purpose flour
3 cups semi-sweet chocolate chips

Preheat oven to 350 degrees. In a large mixing bowl blend together butter, sugars, eggs, baking soda and vanilla. Beat until fluffy. Mix in one half of the flour. Add chocolate chips. Mix in the remaining flour. Place balls of dough on a non-stick cookie sheet or jelly roll pan. Bake at 350 degrees for 10 to 12 minutes or until golden brown.
Yield: 5 dozen cookies

## Herb Feta Frittata

❖ *This Frittata recipe is for a low fat product. It can be prepared with whole eggs and regular half and half and whole milk.*

2 teaspoons dry minced onion
2 cups Italian blend cheese, shredded
3 tablespoons herb feta cheese
2 tablespoons all-purpose flour
1/8 teaspoon baking powder
1 cup egg substitute
2 whole eggs
1/4 teaspoon garlic, chopped
1 cup fat free half and half
2/3 cup non-fat milk

Preheat oven to 350 degrees. Spray a 10-inch pie plate with non-stick cooking spray. Place dry onion, and cheeses in bottom of dish. In a blender beat flour, baking powder, egg substitute, eggs, garlic, half and half, and non-fat milk. Pour liquid over cheese in pie plate. Bake for 45 to 60 minutes at 350 degrees, until frittata is set.
Yield: 4 to 6 servings

## Chile and Tomato Cheese Strata

2 cups liquid egg substitute or 8 whole eggs
1 1/2 cups non-fat half and half
1 1/2 cups one percent low fat milk
3 tablespoons dry mustard
2 cups low fat cheese
1 can (4 ounces) diced chilies, drained
1 can (8 ounces) diced tomatoes, drained
1 loaf French bread, torn into pieces

Coat a 9 x 13 inch pan with non-stick cooking spray. In blender combine egg substitute, milk, nonfat half and half and mustard. Set aside. Place most of the bread in bottom of pan. Sprinkle with 1 1/2 cups of the cheese. Place remaining bread without crust on top. Cover with remaining cheese. Pour egg mixture over bread. Sprinkle chilies and tomatoes over top. Cover and refrigerate over night. Bake for 1 hour at 350 degrees until center is set.
Yield: 6 to 8 servings

❖ *This recipe has been perfected over 25 years. It is now a signature recipe of the Beazley House.*

❖ *This is a low-fat, low cholesterol dish. It can be prepared with whole eggs, regular half and half, whole milk and regular fat cheese if desired.*

❖ *Low-fat cheddar, mozzarella or cheese may be used.*

## Pumpkin Bread

1 tablespoon canola oil
1 cup sugar
1/2 cup applesauce
2 small eggs
1 teaspoon vanilla
1 cup canned pumpkin
1 cup all-purpose flour
1/2 tablespoon baking soda
1/2 teaspoon baking powder
1/2 teaspoon cinnamon
3/4 teaspoon all spice
1/8 teaspoon ground cloves
1/2 cup low fat buttermilk
1 cup all-purpose flour
1 cup raisins
1/4 cup almonds, chopped.

❖ *Fresh pumpkin may be substituted for canned.*

❖ *Pumpkin bread is great served any season.*

Preheat oven to 325 degrees. In a large bowl blend oil, sugar, applesauce, eggs, vanilla and pumpkin. Add 1 cup flour, baking soda, baking powder, cinnamon, all spice and cloves. Mix until smooth. Add buttermilk, remaining 1 cup flour, raisins and almonds. Mix well. Spray large bundt pan with non-stick cooking spray. Fill pan 2/3 full of batter. Bake at 325 for 45 minutes until wooden pick inserted in center comes out clean.

Yield: approximately 16 servings

## Daughter's Inn

The Daughter's Inn is owned by Carol and Jim Beazley and is near the Beazley House. The two bed and breakfasts are operated as one entity. The guests at the Daughters Inn have their breakfast at the Beazley House. The garden is shared by both.

This house has a much different history then the Beazley House. It has had many different owners. The home started out in 1902 as a Queen Anne Victorian style with turrets and a veranda. In the early 1920's it was changed into a California bungalow. The house was stuccoed, the turrets were removed, and porches were added across the front and side of the house.

The inside of the house was painted a pale pea green. This color was often found in hospitals and clinics and indeed this home was owned by a psychiatrist, who had his practice in the home. He owned the home for 22 years. Fortunately some of the inside features were preserved. The original hardwood floors and the coved ceilings were intact. The beautiful tile fireplace in the parlor was painted but could be restored.

Carol and Jim purchased the house in 2001 and set about the renovation of the home. Two years later it was ready to be opened as a bed and breakfast. The house was given an award of merit by Napa Landmarks for the rehabilitation and adaptive reuse as a historic structure.

## Chili and Cheese Strata

2 cups liquid egg substitute
1 1/2 cups non-fat half and half
1 1/2 cups non-fat milk
3 teaspoons dry mustard
1 loaf French bread, torn into pieces
2 cups low fat cheese blends, shredded (Italian, cheddar, mozzarella)
1 tablespoon onion, minced
1 can (4 ounces) diced chilies.

*This is a low fat recipe and can be prepared with whole eggs, whole half and half and whole milk if desired.*

*Strata can be baked after assembling and served immediately if desired.*

In blender combine egg substitute, half and half, milk and mustard. Blend until smooth. Layer half of bread in bottom of 9 x 13 inch pan coated with non-stick cooking spray. Sprinkle half of cheese over bread. Add onions and chilies. Layer remaining bread on top. Sprinkle remaining cheese on bread. Pour blender mixture over entire strata. Cover and refrigerate overnight. Bake at 350 degrees for 1 hour until golden brown and center is set.
Yield: 12 servings

## Fiesta Bean Bake

1 can (16 ounces) Mexican style chili beans or black beans
1 can (16 ounces) whole kernel corn, drained
1 can (16 ounces) diced tomatoes with liquid
1 can (7 ounces) green chilies, chopped
1 can (4 ounces) black olives, sliced
3 cups egg substitute
8 small corn tortillas, torn into bite size pieces
8 ounces cheddar cheese, shredded
3/4 cup fat free half and half
1/2 cup salsa
Taco seasoning to taste

*Serve with salsa and sour cream.*

*Monterey Jack cheese can be substituted for cheddar cheese.*

Preheat oven to 350 degrees. In large bowl mix all ingredients. Coat 9 x 12 inch baking dish with cooking spray. Pour mixture into baking dish. Bake for 30 to 45 minutes at 350 degrees.
Yield: 9 to 12 servings

## Mandarin Orange Bread Pudding

1 loaf French bread, torn into pieces
1 can (11 ounces) mandarin oranges
1/2 cup orange juice
2 cups non-fat milk
Liquid from mandarin oranges
2 cups liquid egg substitute
1 teaspoon orange extract
1 teaspoon orange zest
1/3 cup sugar

Preheat oven to 350 degrees. Drain mandarin oranges and save liquid. Place bread in 9 x 13 inch baking pan sprayed with non-stick cooking spray. Scatter mandarin orange segments over bread. In a blender mix orange juice, non-fat milk, mandarin orange liquid, egg substitute, orange extract, orange zest and sugar. Pour blender mixture over bread. Bake for 45 to 55 minutes at 350 degrees until golden brown and the center is set.
Yield: 6 to 8 servings

❖ *This is a low fat recipe. It can be prepared with whole eggs and whole milk if desired.*

❖ *After combining all ingredients the Mandarin Orange Bread Pudding can be refrigerated over night and baked off in the morning if desired.*

## Blueberry Coffee Cake

2 cups all-purpose flour
3/4 cup sugar
2 1/2 teaspoons baking powder
1/4 cup butter, melted
3/4 cup buttermilk
1/2 cup vanilla yogurt
1 egg
2 cups fresh or frozen blueberries

❖ *Blueberry Coffee Cake is done when wooden pick inserted in center comes out clean.*

Preheat oven to 350 degrees. In mixing bowl combine all ingredients except blueberries. Mix to blend. Carefully fold in blueberries. Pour into bundt pan. Sprinkle with crumble. Bake for 45 to 50 minutes at 350 degrees.
Yield: 12 to 16 servings

## Crumble Topping
3/4 cup all-purpose flour
1/2 cup brown sugar, packed
1/2 teaspoon cinnamon
1/2 cup cold butter or margarine

In small bowl combine flour, sugar and cinnamon. Cut butter into mixture until crumbly. Sprinkle over blueberry coffee cake.
Yield: 1 1/4 cups

## Napa Inn

In the dining room of the Napa Inn is a small table holding beautiful Cranberry Glass plates, a bowl and lamp. When I met Brooke Boyer, she and her husband own the Inn, I asked about the crystal. She told me she had the antique Cranberry Glass before she opened the Inn. I thought how appropriate that the furnishings of the Inn seem to fit so well with the Cranberry Glass.

This 100 year old home was given to Madeline "Minnie" Migliavacca and Harry Lewis Johnston as a wedding gift from his father. In May 1899 the Napa Daily Journal reported "the house was built by the building contractor, E.A. Wright for $3,091.00." It further stated "the home was to be a seven room residence for Harry Johnston, which will be erected on First Street. The house will be in the Colonial style, two stories in height, with a seven-foot basement. On the first floor will be a reception hall, parlor, dining room, kitchen and pantry. The second story will contain three bedrooms. The attic will be finished. The house will be heated by hot air and gas."

After the honeymoon, the Johnston's moved into their new home and resided there during their 50 years of marriage. They did not have children. Both Minnie and Harry were active in the Napa community. Harry was the senior partner in the law firm of Harry L. and Leslie E. Johnston, his younger brother. They represented the bank, railroad and water companies in Napa as well as private clients.

In November 1949 just a few months after the Johnston's fiftieth wedding anniversary, 80 year old Harry passed away. Minnie also completed her life at the First Street residence on June 15, 1961.

The house was willed to the city of Napa. Over the next 16 years the house was used as municipal office space and also as a rental. In 1974 it was briefly used by the police department. The police department decided to build a larger building and tear down the Johnston house. Tom Connell came to the rescue and bought the house. He had the 170 ton building moved to Warren Street. Mr. Connell's mother lived in the house and started a bed and breakfast in 1981.

The home went through several owners before James and Brooke Boyer purchased it in 1998 and opened their bed and breakfast. They also purchased the Buford house in September 1999. The two buildings operate as one entity. The breakfast is served in the large dining room of the Napa Inn. There is a shared large parking area behind the buildings.

## Granola

5 cups uncooked old fashioned oatmeal
1 cup sunflower seeds raw, unsalted
1/2 cup sesame seeds, raw
1/2 cup coconut, shredded
1 cup almonds, sliced
1/2 tablespoon cinnamon
1/2 cup vegetable oil
3/4 cup honey
2 tablespoons water
1 1/4 teaspoons vanilla
1/2 cup raisins
1/4 cup dried cranberries
1/4 cup dried apricots, chopped

❖ *It may be necessary to bake in several batches so all the mixture can be baked until golden brown.*

❖ *Store in airtight container or in plastic freezer bags.*

Preheat oven to 300 degrees. In a large bowl mix oatmeal, sunflower seeds, sesame seeds, coconut, almonds and cinnamon. In small sauce pan combine oil, honey and water. Heat until blended. Add vanilla. Pour oil and honey mixture over dry ingredients. Mix well. Place mixture in baking dish and bake for 10 minutes at 300 degrees until granola is golden brown. Remove from oven and add raisins, cranberries and apricots. Cool.
Yield: approximately 8 cups

## Fresh Vegetable Quiche

1 1/2 tablespoons vegetable oil
3/4 cup mushrooms, chopped
3/4 cup zucchini, sliced
1/3 cup green onions, chopped
3/4 cup bell peppers, sliced
1 tablespoon dried onion flakes
1/2 teaspoon seasoning salt
1/2 teaspoon ground black pepper
9 eggs
3/4 cup half and half cream
6 ounces cream cheese
1 cup cheddar cheese, shredded
3/4 cup croutons

❖ *Quiche pan can be used for this recipe.*

❖ *Recipe can be cut into half for smaller number of servings.*

Preheat oven to 350 degrees. Heat oil in skillet. Sauté vegetables and seasonings until soft. Spread over bottom of greased 8 x 11 inch baking dish. In mixing bowl mix eggs, half and half cream and cheeses together. Pour over vegetables. Top with croutons. Bake for 1 hour at 350 degrees until center is set.
Yield: 6 to 8 servings

❖ *Suggested wine pairing - Dry Rosé*

## Cranberry Almond Scones

3/4 cup all-purpose flour
2 tablespoons sugar
3/4 cup oatmeal
1 1/2 teaspoon baking powder
1/2 teaspoon cream of tarter
1/4 cup almonds, sliced
1/4 cup dried cranberries
Zest of 1 orange
1 egg
3 tablespoons milk
4 tablespoons butter, melted

❖ *Many different dried fruits can be substituted for the cranberries.*

Preheat oven to 375 degrees. In mixing bowl combine flour, sugar, oatmeal, baking powder, and cream of tarter,. Add almonds, cranberries and orange zest.  In separate bowl mix egg and milk. Add egg mixture to dry ingredients. Add butter. Knead dough until it holds together. Spoon onto greased cookie sheet. Bake for 15 to 20 minutes at 375 degrees. Let cool for 20 minutes before serving.

Yield: 6 scones

# English Scones

1/4 cup currants
1 tablespoon brandy
Zest of 1 orange
2 cups all-purpose flour
6 tablespoons sugar
1 tablespoon baking powder
1/4 teaspoon salt
1/2 cup butter
1/2 cup plus 2 teaspoons buttermilk
1/2 teaspoon sugar

Preheat oven to 400 degrees. In microwave safe bowl mix currants, brandy and orange peel. Heat in microwave on high for 1 minute. In separate bowl mix flour, sugar, baking powder and salt. Using a pastry blender cut butter into flour mixture until lumps are approximately 1/4 inch in size. Stir in currant mixture. Add 1/2 cup buttermilk. Stir just enough to moisten dough. If crumbly sprinkle more buttermilk over mixture and stir. Pat dough into ball and knead in bowl until it holds together. Set dough on lightly greased 12 x 15 inch baking sheet. Flatten into 1/2 inch thick round. With floured knife cut round into quarters or eights leaving wedges in place. Brush top with remaining 2 teaspoons buttermilk and sprinkle with 1/2 teaspoon sugar. Bake for 20 to 25 minutes at 400 degrees until golden brown.
Yield: 4 to 8 servings

❖ *This recipe can be reduced for smaller number of scones.*

## Pear Tarte

**Filling**
1 can (16 ounces) pear halves, drained
1/2 cup sour cream
1 egg yolk
1/4 cup brown sugar

Preheat oven to 350 degrees. Spread streusel in baking dish. Place pears on top of streusel. In a small bowl mix sour cream, egg yolk and brown sugar. Pour over pears. Bake for 20 to 30 minutes at 350 degrees.
Yield: 6 servings

**Streusel**
1 1/2 cups all-purpose flour
1/2 cup sugar
1/2 cup brown sugar
3/4 teaspoon nutmeg
3/4 teaspoon cinnamon
3/4 teaspoon salt
3/4 cup butter

In medium bowl combine all ingredients until mixture appears as course breadcrumbs.
Yield: 3 cups

❖ *Try canned peaches or apricots for different variations.*

❖ *Suggested wine pairings -*
   *Muscato*
   *Muscat*

## *Buford House*

The Buford House was built in 1877 by Simeon Buford, a wealthy Berryessa rancher. He built this large Monte Chilo house as a town house. His wife died in 1896 leaving him with three grandchildren. By 1900 his daughter Helen, called Maud, was living in the house with her father and her three children. In June of 1900 she died of an overdose of laudanum poisoning.

The Napa Register newspaper described this incident. "About 1 o'clock Tuesday afternoon Maud Baxter asked her servant to darken her room and take the children downstairs to keep them quiet so she might sleep. A few minutes later Dr. Hennessey called and going to her room found her unconscious and breathing heavy. Her condition alarmed him and he at once sent for Dr. Hann. He attempted to revive her but she expired within a very few minutes. The theory of the Doctor and of the Coroner's jury who heard the evidence was that, suffering from great pain and fatigue from insomnia she took a dose of laudanum, but accidentally took too much."

Simeon's son Kirtley was a well known rancher and spent time in San Francisco. He was noted for saving a man's life. According to the records at that time he received a good deal of well-merited praise from those who witnessed the incident.

In 1908 Kirtley was visiting friends in San Francisco and became ill. He died three days later of typhoid fever at the age of 35. Three days later Simeon disappeared and was never heard from again.

From 1920 to 1955 the house was used by Napa County as a youth detention center. Mary Arnold, living nearby on Calistoga Avenue would watch the "detained" and felt sorry for their lack of equipment with which to play. At her death she left a trust fund to buy appropriate amenities for the children. Some time later the house was used for 4-H activities.

When the house was condemned by the city Tom Connell bought the home. It became an apartment building before it became a bed and breakfast.

Brooke and Jim Boyer purchased the Buford House in 1999 and renovated the entire building in 2001 and 2002 to make 8 guest rooms. In 2002 one of the rooms, William's Hideaway (named after Brooke's father) was redecorated on the TV show Trading Spaces. It aired on April 30, 2005.

## Hash Brown Quiche

1 1/2 to 2 pounds hash brown potatoes (7 to 10 cups potatoes)
1 teaspoon ground black pepper
1 teaspoon seasoned salt
2 tablespoons dried onion flakes
1 teaspoon garlic powder
1 teaspoon garlic and herb seasoning
1/2 cup butter, melted
1 cup jalapeno cheese, shredded
1 cup Monterey Jack cheese, shredded
1 cup cheddar cheese, shredded
1 cup cooked ham, diced
1 cup milk
3 eggs
1 tomato, chopped
2 tablespoons fresh basil, chopped

❖ *The hash brown quiche can be partially prepared the night before serving and completed in the morning. After combining the potatoes, seasonings and butter, refrigerate until morning.*

*In the morning complete the recipe.*

Preheat oven to 350 degrees. In a large mixing bowl combine potatoes, seasonings and butter. Pour mixture into greased 8 x 11 inch baking pan. Bake for 30 minutes at 350 degrees. Remove from oven. In a separate bowl combine cheeses and ham. Spread over the top of the hash browns. Beat milk and eggs together and pour over cheeses and potato mixture. Return to oven and bake for 20 minutes. Spread tomato and basil over top and bake for an additional 10 to 15 minutes.
Yield: 10 servings

## Apricot Shortbread

1/2 cup (1 stick) butter, at room temperature
1 cup all-purpose flour
1/3 cup sugar
1 1/2 cups dried apricots, coarsely chopped
1 egg, beaten
1/4 cup water, from soaking apricots
1/2 cup sugar
1/3 cup all-purpose flour
1/4 teaspoon salt
1/2 teaspoon baking powder
Powdered sugar

### Crust

Preheat oven to 350 degrees. In mixing bowl combine butter, 1 cup flour and 1/3 cup sugar. Blend with spoon or hands until smooth. Pat dough evenly over bottom of 9-inch pie dish. Bake for 25 minutes at 350 degrees.

### Filling

To make filling, place dried apricots in hot water and let stand over night. Drain softened apricots, reserving 1/4 cup liquid. Place apricots in mixing bowl and add egg. Mix well. Add reserved apricot liquid, sugar, flour, salt and baking powder. Beat until smooth. Spread apricot mixture over crust and bake for 35 minutes at 350 degrees, until puffy and lightly browned on top. Remove from oven, cool slightly and shake powdered sugar over the top. Cut into wedges.
Yield: 12 servings

❖ *If using fresh apricots, cook with water on high, reduce heat to medium, stirring often.*

❖ *Add more sugar to apricots if necessary.*

## Herb Cheese

8 ounces cream cheese
3/4 teaspoon garlic powder
2 sprigs fresh parsley, chopped or 2 teaspoon dry parsley
1 1/2 tablespoons butter, softened
1/3 teaspoon dried oregano
1/3 teaspoon dried thyme
1/3 teaspoon dried basil
1 teaspoon garlic and herb seasoning
Salt and pepper to taste

In mixing bowl blend all ingredients until smooth. Refrigerate.
Yield: 1 cup

*❖ Other types of cheese can be added in this recipe. Cut the cheese into small pieces and soften in a microwave for 10 seconds before adding to the herb cheese mixture.*

## Sun-Dried Tomato Spread

1 cup herb cheese
3/4 cup sun-dried tomatoes, chopped
2 tablespoons parmesan cheese
1/3 teaspoon paprika
1/3 teaspoon ground black pepper

In mixing bowl combine all ingredients and mix until blended.
Yield: 1 3/4 cups

*❖ The Herb Cheese and the Sun- Dried Tomato Spread will keep in the refrigerator for two weeks.*

## *Hidden Oak Inn*

*I* find the history of the beautiful homes that are now bed and breakfasts interesting. However, often the stories of the people who lived in the home and the changes that had taken place in the home over the years are lost. This is not true for the Hidden Oak Inn on Napa Street in Sonoma.

Valerie Patterson, the present owner of the Hidden Oak Inn has researched the history of the home way back to its beginning in 1914. She has gone through the county and town records, through church files and sought out the past owners for information. In her search for accurate information she was able to add a postcard dated 1913 which was sent to Francis Murphy, daughter of Ralph Murphy, who built this house. During remodeling it was found in a crevice behind the fireplace.

The records show that the house became a boarding home in 1934. Some local teachers and nurses lived in the home. Along about 1946 to 1950 it was owned by the nearby Trinity Episcopal church and was used as a church hall.

In 1969 the James Adams family purchased the home for their large family. While there they made several improvements including adding a bathroom on the second floor. The biggest addition was the swimming pool in the back yard.

The house was owned by Jacque and Barbara Gasser in 1984 and was converted into a bed and breakfast – one of the first in Sonoma. They kept the home and operated the bed and breakfast for four years, then it was sold to Catherine Cotchette in May of 1988. Catherine made some additional changes to the home for the guests' comfort.

In 1999 Valerie Patterson and her husband moved from Texas to Sonoma. They had never thought of owning and running a bed and breakfast. Valerie is a registered nurse and a stay-at-home mother. It was more or less her responsibility to find a home for the family because her husband's job required that he travel a great deal. When the Hidden Oak Inn came on the market she was pleased to find a home close to a school for her son with the opportunity of a job that would keep her at home. Valerie loves to cook so it didn't take long to realize a bed and breakfast was a perfect fit.

When I came to visit the Hidden Oak Inn it was under complete renovation. Everything was being changed to meet the latest code standards and to create space for needed services. Located just blocks from Sonoma's Historic Plaza, this California Craftsman Bungalow creates a comfortable feeling for the guests.

## Mandarin Salad

1 head romaine lettuce
2 cups baby spinach
3 green onions, sliced thin
1 can (8 ounces) mandarin oranges, drained
1/4 cup dried cranberries
1/2 cup sugar coated almonds, sliced
1/4 cup crispy wonton noodles

❖ *Adding grilled chicken breasts makes this salad a delightful summer entree.*

Tear lettuce into bite-size pieces. Place in salad bowl. Add spinach, green onions, oranges and cranberries. Add dressing and mix well. Sprinkle with almonds and wonton noodles just before serving.
Yield: 8 to 10 servings

❖ *Suggested wine pairing - Sauvignon Blanc*

### Sweet and Sour Dressing
1/4 cup rice wine vinegar
1/8 to 1/4 cup sugar
2 tablespoons fresh basil, snipped
1 clove garlic, minced
1/2 teaspoon salt
1/4 teaspoon pepper
1/2 cup vegetable oil

In blender combine vinegar, sugar, basil, garlic, salt and pepper. With blender running, pour oil into blender to emulsify. Chill for 2 to 4 hours to blend flavors.
Yield: 1 cup

### Sugar Coated Almonds
1/2 cup sliced almonds
Sugar to coat

Place almonds in skillet. Sprinkle with sugar. Cook over low heat until sugar melts and almonds are coated, stirring constantly. Pour onto wax paper to cool. Break apart and set aside.
Yield: 1/2 cup

## Strawberry Bread

1 1/2 cups all-purpose flour
1 teaspoon cinnamon
1/2 teaspoon baking soda
1/2 teaspoon salt
1/2 cup plus 2 tablespoons vegetable oil
1/2 teaspoon vanilla
2 small eggs
1 cup sugar
1 pint fresh strawberries, chopped
1/2 cup pecans, chopped

Preheat oven to 350 degrees. In mixing bowl combine flour, cinnamon, baking soda and salt. Set aside. In electric mixer bowl combine oil, vanilla, eggs and sugar. Mix well. Gradually add dry ingredients to creamed mixture, stirring just until all ingredients are moistened. Stir in strawberries and pecans. Spoon mixture into greased and floured loaf pan. Bake for 1 hour at 350 degrees, until wooden pick inserted in center comes out clean. Cool in pan for 10 minutes. Remove from pan and cool on wire rack.
Yield: 1 loaf

❖ *1 package (10 ounces) frozen strawberries can be substituted for fresh berries. Thaw and drain berries before using.*

## Sweet Potato Casserole

2 to 3 fresh yams boiled, peeled and mashed
1/4 cup sugar
2 tablespoons butter, melted
1 egg, beaten
1/2 teaspoon vanilla
Pinch nutmeg

### Topping
1/2 cup coconut, shredded
1/2 cup pecans, chopped
1/4 to 1/2 cup brown sugar
1/4 cup butter, melted
3 tablespoons all-purpose flour

❖ *Fresh yams or sweet potatoes may be used.*

❖ *The yam mixture can be refrigerated before the topping is added. Mixture can be held for 24 hours in refrigerator. Bake for 20 to 30 minutes at 350 degrees. Remove from oven and add topping. Return to oven and bake and additional 30 to 45 minutes at 350 degrees.*

Preheat oven to 350 degrees. In mixing bowl combine the first 6 ingredients. Pour into greased 1 1/2 quart baking dish. In separate bowl combine topping ingredients. Sprinkle topping mixture over sweet potatoes in baking dish. Bake uncovered for 30 to 45 minutes at 350 degrees until lightly browned.
Yield: 6 servings

## Asparagus, Bacon and Goat Cheese Tart

6 slices bacon, cooked, crumbled
1 tablespoon bacon drippings
1 shallot, finely chopped
1 pound fresh asparagus, cut in 1-inch pieces
1/4 pound puff pastry, defrosted
1 cup goat cheese, crumbled
1 tablespoon fresh basil, chopped
1/2 teaspoon salt
1/4 teaspoon pepper
1 egg yolk
1/2 teaspoon water

Preheat oven to 450 degrees. Combine egg yolk and 1/2 teaspoon water for egg wash. In skillet heat bacon fat. Sauté shallots for 1 minute. Add asparagus. Cook over medium heat until asparagus is crisp tender. Remove skillet from heat. Add crumbled bacon. On lightly floured parchment paper, roll puff pastry to a 10 x 16 inch rectangle. Transfer pastry on parchment paper to baking sheet. Leaving 1 inch border around edge of pastry, sprinkle with goat cheese. Spread asparagus, bacon, and shallot mixture evenly over cheese on dough. Sprinkle with basil. Season with salt and pepper. Brush edges of pastry with egg yolk wash. Bake for 20 to 25 minutes at 450 degrees, until pastry is golden brown. Let cool slightly before serving.
Yield: 24 appetizers or 6 sides

❖ *Don't aggravate your goat before milking as it sours the cheese!*

❖ *Suggested wine pairing - Pinot Noir*

## Fruit Stuffed Cornish Hens

1 cup water
1/4 cup butter
1 package (8 ouncs) herb seasoned stuffing mix
1 large apple, cored and chopped
1/2 cup chopped pecans
1/4 cup dried cranberries
1 tablespoon orange zest
1 container (8 ounces) soft cream cheese with chives & onions
4 Cornish hens
1 tablespoon vegetable oil
Kosher salt and pepper

### Stuffing

Heat water and butter in saucepan over medium heat until butter melts. Stir in next five ingredients, cover, reduce heat and simmer for 5 minutes.

### Hens

Preheat oven to 350 degrees. Loosen skin from hens without detaching. Spread cream cheese under skin. Lightly spoon stuffing into cavity of hens and close opening with skewers. Place hens in a large roasting pan with breast side up, brush with oil and sprinkle with salt and pepper. Bake hens at 350 degrees for one hour or until meat thermometer registers 165 degrees. Remove skewers and serve.
Yield: 4 servings

❖ *Stuffing recipe may be doubled — place extra stuffing in pan and bake for 30 minutes at 350 degrees. Garnish with chopped parsley.*

❖ *Suggested wine pairing - Chenin Blanc*

## Thistle Dew Inn

The Thistle Dew Inn is actually two houses on the same lot. The house that is now at the rear of the property was built in 1869. The house in the front was on a lot around the corner and was moved to its new site in 1980. It was built in 1910 toward the end of the Victorian period. The house has had several owners over the years.

Jon and Jackie Early purchased the property at the time it was moved and filled it with museum quality Arts and Crafts furnishings. Much of the furniture in the Inn is collector quality quarter-sawn Arts and Crafts furniture designed in the early 20th century by such craftsmen as Gustav Stickley, L. and J. G. Stickley and Charles Limbert. The Arts and Crafts movement which had it's origin in England and in the work of William Morris, was a reaction against the Industrial Revolution and mass produced goods which threatened handcrafted works. I was pleased to see the long oval oak table and the chairs by Gustav Stickley in the dining room. The chairs around the table were actually crafted by Gustav's son. As you enter the front hall there is a unique wall-hung coat tree. The side board and the settee are also very valuable pieces by Gustav Stickley.

The Thistle Dew Inn was the first bed and breakfast licensed in Sonoma and has been in operation since 1981. Mary and "Sunny" Adams took over the operation in 1986 and added additional bathrooms and a hot tub. In 1990 Larry and Norma Barnett purchased the Inn and built the second story of the front house as owner's quarters. They also did a major remodeling of the house in the back that was over 100 year old.

The present owners are Jan Rafiq and her brother Gregg Percival who bought the Inn in 2003. Jan lived in San Mateo and was working in Human Resources. Frequently on her commute to work she thought "wouldn't it be nice to have a job where I did not need to leave home?" Over the years she had thought about owning a bed and breakfast. When it was time for a career change she, with the help of her brother, purchased the Thistle Dew Inn. Jan seems to have reached her goal, to live in a nice place, to share her home and to be able to work from home.

Jan has a very capable staff and that makes the running of the Inn less stressful. Pilar has been at the Inn for 17 years and knows it well. She does most of the cooking except for Sunday morning when Jan and Gregg prepare and serve the gourmet meal. Jan and Pilar plan the menu together so there is a variety for all guests, particularly for those who are at the Inn for several days.

## Banana Buckwheat Pancakes

1 cup unbleached all-purpose flour
1 cup quick cooking oatmeal
1 cup buckwheat flour
4 tablespoons baking powder
1 teaspoon baking soda
1 teaspoon salt
1 tablespoon cinnamon
1 cup sour cream
5 eggs
1 cup water
1 cup milk
3 to 4 bananas, sliced

In large bowl mix dry ingredients. Add sour cream, eggs, water and milk. Slice bananas into small pieces. Add to batter. Mix thoroughly. Let batter rest for 30 minutes. Spoon batter onto buttered hot grill. Cook until bubbles form. Turn and cook until brown.
Yield: 8 to 10 servings

❖ *One half cup whole wheat flour and one half cup buckwheat flour can be substituted for the one cup buckwheat flour.*

❖ *If batter becomes too stiff add more liquid.*

❖ *When cooking wait for bubbles to form on top before turning pancake. Be patient, they take a while to cook.*

❖ *Serve with REAL maple syrup.*

## Three Rice Salad

1 1/2 cups water
1/4 cup long grain white rice
1/4 cup brown rice
1/4 cup wild rice
1 teaspoon lemon zest
1 tablespoon lemon juice
3 tablespoons olive oil
3 tablespoons raisins
1 large carrot, shredded
Salt and pepper to taste

Place water in large sauce pan. Bring to a boil. Add rice. Cook covered until liquid is absorbed and rice is tender. Drain rice and rinse in cold water. Place rice in large bowl. Add remaining ingredients, one at a time, stirring after each addition.
Yield: 4 to 6 servings

❖ *Chill before serving.*

## Cranberry Salsa

1 bag (12 ounces) fresh cranberries
1 quart water
1 clove garlic, minced
1 jalapeno chili, seeded, minced
4 tablespoons cilantro, chopped
3 green onions, chopped
Juice of 3 limes
1/2 cup sugar
Salt and pepper to taste

Boil cranberries in 1 quart water for 1 minute. Drain well. Add remaining ingredients. Stir and mash some of the whole cranberries. Refrigerate until serving.
Yield: approximately 2 cups

❖ *Salsa is a little sweet, a little sour and a little spicy.*

❖ *For a hotter salsa add more jalapeno pepper.*

❖ *This is a great appetizer to serve during the holiday season.*

## Honey Butter

1/2 cup (1 stick) butter
1/2 cup honey

❖ *The flavor of the honey butter will vary according to the flavor of the honey.*

In small sauce pan melt butter. Slowly add honey. Heat, stirring constantly until warm and smooth. Cool slightly before serving.
Yield: 1 cup

## Homemade Applesauce

❖ *Serve with dollop of whipped cream.*

❖ *Add a dash of cinnamon to the whipped cream.*

❖ *Sprinkle with granola for a crust-less apple pie effect.*

6 fresh apples, 2 Granny Smith, 2 Red Delicious and 2 Fuji apples
1/2 cup apple cider

Peel, core and cut apples into small chunks. Place in large sauce pan. Add apple cider. Cook until apples turn to mush with some larger pieces still in mix. Stir occasionally, until uniformly cooked.
Yield: 5 to 6 cups

## Quick and Tasty Artichoke Dip

❖ *Serve hot or cold with crackers, baguette slices or Crackle bread.*

❖ *Dip will keep for several days refrigerated.*

2 small jars (6.5 ounces each) marinated artichoke hearts
1/2 cup mayonnaise
1/2 cup parmesan cheese, shredded

Preheat oven to 350 degrees. Drain and chop artichoke hearts. Place in bowl. Add mayonnaise and cheese. Mix well. Spoon mixture into small baking/serving dish. Sprinkle more cheese on top. Bake for 20 minutes at 350 degrees.
Yield: 2 1/2 cups

## Dutch Babies

1/4 cup unbleached all-purpose flour
1/8 cup water
1/8 cup milk
1/4 teaspoon salt
2 eggs
2 tablespoons ricotta cheese
Drop of vanilla
1 teaspoon sugar
1 tablespoon jam or jelly

Preheat oven to 500 degrees. In mixing bowl combine all ingredients except cheese, vanilla, sugar and jam. Spray oil on individual 6-inch baking dish. Pour batter into dish, about 1/2 inch deep. Bake for 10 to 12 minutes at 500 degrees, until puffed and brown on top. Remove from oven. Remove from baking dish and place on serving plate. In small bowl, combine cheese, vanilla and sugar. Warm slightly in microwave. Spoon warmed cheese mixture onto middle of Dutch Baby. Place jam or jelly in center of cheese. Sprinkle with powdered sugar.
Yield: 1 serving

❖ *Use different kinds of jam or jelly with the Dutch Babies for variety.*

❖ *Oven must be very hot.*

❖ *Dutch Babies must be served immediately after baking. They do not hold well after baking.*

❖ *Some topping variations include: lemon curd, stewed dried fruit and apple sauce.*

❖ *Recipe may be increased as needed.*

❖ *Fresh strawberries may be substituted for the jam or jelly.*

# Tortellini Salad

❖ *One half teaspoon dried dill can be substituted for the fresh dill.*

❖ *Suggested wine pairing - Dry Rosé*

1 package (20 ounces) fresh cheese tortellini
2 cloves garlic, minced
1/4 cup onion, chopped
1 tablespoon fresh dill
5 sun-dried tomatoes in olive oil
1 tablespoon capers
1/2 cup parmesan cheese, grated
5 tablespoons olive oil
2 tablespoons rice wine vinegar

Cook tortellini until firm tender. Rinse with cold water. In large bowl combine garlic, onion, capers, tomatoes and dill. Add tortellini. Add cheese, oil and vinegar. Refrigerate until serving.
Yield: 8 to 10 servings

## A Captain's House

The land of the Larson Family Winery has a long history going back to 1834 when the young Lt. Mariano G. Vallejo passed through on his way to the mission, San Francisco Solano de Sonoma, last and northmost of the 21 California missions. Vallejo established the town of Sonoma that was for many years, socially and politically superior to Yerba Buena, the little town 50 miles south now called San Francisco. It was the Embarcadero, farthest navigable point up Sonoma Creek from the San Francisco Bay. Small craft landed European visitors and influential people from San Francisco on the landing that is now the Larsen Family Winery. Passengers and freight bound for Sonoma transferred here from sloops and schooners to horse and ox-drawn carriages and wagons for the ride to the Plaza in Sonoma.

Beginning in 1847 steamboats docked and turned around for the voyage back to San Francisco. One of the steamboat captains built a captain's house, the Civil War era farm house that still stands today. The banister is said to be make from a ships mast. Today "A Captain's House" is a rental vacation home.

Tom Larson's great grandfather, Michael Millerick bought the house and the 101 acres of land in 1890. It has been in the family for 5 generations.

The Millerick Ranch was the site for the Sonoma Rodeo from 1929 to 1950. It was the largest and longest running rodeo in the Bay area. Attracting up to 8,000 people who dined on beef roasted in underground pits. World champions, "hall of famers" and local cowboys competed for the trophies. One year, vintner August Sebastiani won a roping trophy.

On the site of their family's old Sonoma Rodeo where rodeo stock, racehorses and polo ponies once grazed Tom Larson and his father, Bob decided to plant Chardonnay grapes in 1977. Tom earned his degree in fermentation science from the University California at Davis. The business grew and soon they were distributing wine to Safeway Stores and many other outlets.

In 1990 Tom and his wife Becky purchased the farm from Tom's father. A few years ago Becky made the transition from a nearly 20-year Silicon Valley career as one of the countries top recruiters to running the winery with Tom. In her role she wears many hats. She is responsible for the rental vacation home and the guests that visit. Advertising and public relations are two professions that she excels in for she is charismatic, charming and very knowledgeable. It was a delight to visit with her. I am sure all the guests delight in meeting her.

## Barbeque Salmon Filets

2 pounds boneless, skinless salmon filets
Barbeque Sauce

❖ *Serve cilantro sauce on top of cooked salmon as it comes off the grill (see recipe on page 113).*

❖ *Extra cilantro sauce can be served with the salmon.*

❖ *Suggested wine pairing - Pinot Noir*

Coat salmon fillets generously with barbeque sauce and set aside for 20 minutes. Grill over "hot" fire for 3 to 4 minutes on each side so outside of fish and sauce gets a slight char but inside remains moist and flaky. Brush with additional sauce while grilling.
Yield: 6 servings

## Barbeque Sauce

1 cup catsup
1 cup honey
1/3 cup dry mustard
1/4 cup rice wine vinegar
2 large jalapeno peppers, finely minced
1 tablespoon hot sauce
4 tablespoons dark brown sugar
3 tablespoons molasses
2 tablespoons curry powder
2 tablespoons paprika
1 tablespoon soy sauce
5 cloves garlic, finely minced
1 tablespoon vegetable oil
1 tablespoon Worcestershire sauce
Juice of 1 lemon
1 teaspoon ground black pepper.

In sauce pan combine all ingredients. Stir to blend. Simmer over medium to medium-low heat for 20 minutes, stirring occasionally to prevent burning.
Yield: approximately 3 cups

## Marinated Mango and Brie Quesadilla

4 flour tortillas, 10-inch diameter
1 ripe mango, peeled, sliced thin
2 tablespoons Gewürztraminer wine
8 ounces brie, sliced thin
3 scallions, sliced
1/2 cup fresh cilantro, chopped
1 Serrano or jalapeno chile, diced with seeds

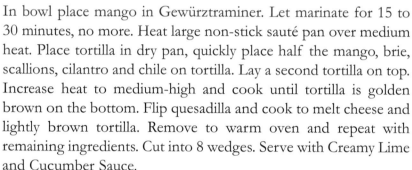

In bowl place mango in Gewürztraminer. Let marinate for 15 to 30 minutes, no more. Heat large non-stick sauté pan over medium heat. Place tortilla in dry pan, quickly place half the mango, brie, scallions, cilantro and chile on tortilla. Lay a second tortilla on top. Increase heat to medium-high and cook until tortilla is golden brown on the bottom. Flip quesadilla and cook to melt cheese and lightly brown tortilla. Remove to warm oven and repeat with remaining ingredients. Cut into 8 wedges. Serve with Creamy Lime and Cucumber Sauce.
Yield: 6 to 8 servings

### Creamy Lime and Cucumber Sauce

1/3 cup sour cream
2 tablespoons squeezed lime juice
1/4 teaspoon salt
Half cucumber, diced

In bowl mix sour cream, lime juice and salt. Gently add cucumber, stir. Serve sauce with quesadillas.
Yield: 3/4 to 1 cup

❖ *Pair this with a bottle of Larson Family Winery 2004 Estate Gewürztraminer for a great summer appetizer.*

❖ *Place dollop of sauce in center of cooked quesadilla and top with a little cilantro.*

❖ *Serve extra sauce on the side of the quesadilla.*

**A Captain's House**

## Cilantro Sauce

2 tablespoons malt or white vinegar
2 tablespoons honey
1 to 2 bunches fresh cilantro, chopped
1 shallot, finely chopped
1 cup premium grade extra virgin olive oil

❖ *Serve Cilantro Sauce with salmon and seafood dishes.*

Combine all ingredients except oil in blender. Add oil in thin steady stream while blending, allowing ingredients to emulsify. Scrape sides of blender. Blend until sauce is thick and well blended.
Yield: 1 1/2 cups

## Roast Rack of Lamb

2 to 3 pound rack of lamb

❖ *For olive oil we suggest using Larson Family Winery Damn Good Olive Oil.*

### Marinade
1/2 teaspoon salt
1/2 teaspoon ground black pepper
4 cloves garlic, minced
3 tablespoons French-style mustard
2 tablespoons soy sauce
2 teaspoons rosemary, chopped
3 tablespoons squeezed lemon juice
1/4 cup olive oil
1/8 cup Pinot Noir

❖ *For wine we suggest using Larson Family Winery Carneros Pinot Noir.*

Preheat oven to 425 degrees. In small bowl mash salt, pepper and garlic together. Whisk in mustard, soy sauce, rosemary, lemon juice, oil and wine. Place lamb in marinade and refrigerate for 8 hours, turning occasionally to coat. Roast rack of lamb in aluminum roasting pan for 20 to 25 minutes at 425 degrees.
Yield: 3 to 4 servings

*Trojan Horse Inn*

The Farrell family owned a lumber yard and the land around the yard back in 1887. Mr. Farrell built this large wooden house as a family home and as a show place for his lumber. The Farrell family apparently lived in the home until 1984 when it was sold. The new owners converted the home into a bed and breakfast. Since that time there has been 6 owners.

In March of 2004 Greg and Bethany Johns left the corporate world of New York City to own and operate a bed and breakfast in the Wine Country. Over the years they had stayed at many bed and breakfasts and had thought about owning one. Before buying the Trojan Horse Inn they had done extensive research. They recognized that the Wine Country in Northern California drew many visitors each year and many would be interested in staying at a bed and breakfast. Before buying they checked out bed and breakfasts in St. Helena, Calistoga, Napa and others in nearby towns. The Trojan Horse met their criteria for an inn. It was large enough and had adequate parking. The area not only had wineries but had hiking and biking trails.

Greg and Bethany set about remodeling the home. This included repainting the walls, installing new floors, changing the furniture and curtains. The renovation was extensive and brought about a fresh new look. There is unique antique furniture in some of the rooms.

Greg and Bethany brought their own china and etched glass crystal for use at the Inn.

Greg does most of the cooking with help from Bethany. Cooking has always been a hobby of his. I asked if he had a favorite type of cooking and he shared with me that he really enjoyed the preparation of all types of foods.

## Maple Corn Muffins

1 cup all-purpose flour
1/2 cup yellow corn meal
1/2 tablespoon baking powder
1/2 teaspoon salt
1 large egg
2 tablespoons brown sugar, packed
1/2 cup milk
3 tablespoons pure maple syrup
2 1/2 tablespoons butter, melted

Preheat oven to 350 degrees. In large bowl combine flour, corn meal, baking powder and salt. In separate bowl whisk egg and brown sugar until smooth. Add milk and maple syrup. Whisk to mix. Pour mixture over dry ingredients. Add melted butter. Fold with spatula just until dry ingredients are moistened. Scoop batter into greased muffin cups, until nearly full. Bake for 25 to 30 minutes at 350 degrees, until golden brown and firm in the center. Let cool in cups on wire rack for 5 minutes.
Yield: 6 muffins

## Pears Poached in Red Wine

❖ *Bosc pears and Anjou pears are good choices for this recipe.*

❖ *Remove pears from sauce with slotted spoon. Transfer each half into one of 8 shallow bowls. Pour a little sauce over each.*

❖ *Serve warm or chilled.*

3 cups (approx. 1 bottle) dry red wine
1/2 cup sugar
1/2 teaspoon lemon zest
4 whole cloves
1 cinnamon stick, cracked
8 black peppercorns
1/2 teaspoon vanilla
4 firm ripe pears, peeled, halved, stemmed and seeded

In a large sauce pan combine wine, sugar, lemon zest, cloves, cinnamon, peppercorns and vanilla. Bring to a boil. Cook to reduce by half. Add pears. Simmer for 20 minutes. Strain sauce through fine mesh.
Yield: 8 servings

# Cinnamon Chip Scones

2 cups all-purpose flour
1/3 cup sugar
1 tablespoon baking powder
1/2 teaspoon salt
1 cup cinnamon chips
6 tablespoons cold butter, cut into cubes
3/4 cup heavy cream
2 large egg yolks, slightly beaten

Preheat oven to 400 degrees. In a large bowl whisk flour, sugar, baking powder and salt. Add cinnamon chips. Toss until evenly distributed and coated. Cut butter into flour mixture with pastry cutter to form pieces the size of a pea. In small bowl stir cream and egg yolks until blended. Add to flour mixture. Mix with fork to combine wet ingredients with dry ingredients. Gently knead dough with hands until dough can be formed into moist ball. Do not over-knead. Set the ball on generously greased baking sheet. Pat into round, 1 inch thick and 7 inches diameter. With sharp knife cut the round into 8 wedges. Separate wedges. Brush each with egg-milk glaze. Sprinkle with sugar. Bake for 18 to 22 minutes at 400 degrees, until deep golden and wooden pick inserted in center comes out clean. Place scones on rack and let cool for 10 to 15 minutes before serving.
Yield: 8 servings

❖ *Add more flour if needed.*

❖ *Add egg mixture to dry ingredients all at once.*

❖ *Dough will be sticky but benefits from minimal handling.*

❖ *Do not make round flatter then 1 inch.*

## Glaze for Scones
1 large egg, slightly beaten
1 tablespoon milk
1 teaspoon sugar

In small bowl combine egg and milk until well blended. Brush uncooked scones with egg wash. Sprinkle with sugar.

## Peaches in Soft Brandied Cream

3 large ripe peaches, peeled and sliced
1/2 cup powdered sugar, sifted
1/2 cup heavy cream
3 tablespoons peach brandy
1/2 teaspoon vanilla
Mint sprigs for garnish

❖ *Serve in glass bowls or large wine glasses.*

❖ *Garnish with fresh mint sprigs.*

Place peaches in large bowl. Sprinkle with 1/4 cup powdered sugar. Stir gently to coat slices. Set aside. In mixing bowl beat cream just until peaks begin to form. Add remaining 1/4 cup powdered sugar, peach brandy, and vanilla. Beat until soft peaks form. Fold whipped cream mixture into peaches.
Yield: 6 servings

## Chocolate Pancakes with Chocolate Sauce

1/2 cup Dutch processed unsweetened cocoa powder
1 1/4 cups all-purpose flour
1 cup sugar
1 teaspoon baking soda
1/8 teaspoon salt
2 large eggs
1 large egg yolk
3/4 cup buttermilk, well shaken
1/4 cup whole milk
1/4 cup canola oil
1 teaspoon vanilla

Heat griddle over moderately low heat. Lightly coat with butter. In large mixing bowl sift cocoa, flour, sugar, baking soda and salt. In separate bowl whisk eggs, egg yolk, buttermilk, whole milk, oil and vanilla. Add dry ingredients to milk mixture. Whisk until well combined. Pour 1/4 cup batter onto hot griddle for each pancake. Cook until bubbles appear on the surface, about 1 to 2 minutes. Flip the pancakes with large spatula. Cook until top springs back when gently touched, about 1 minute. Serve with chocolate sauce.
Yield: 4 servings

❖ *Serve pancakes hot, or stack and cover loosely with foil to keep warm until serving.*

❖ *Chocolate sauce can be prepared in advance and kept in refrigerator until use.*

### Chocolate Sauce
1 cup heavy cream
1 cup bittersweet chocolate, finely chopped

In one quart sauce pan place cream. Bring to boil. Place chocolate in bowl. Pour hot cream over chocolate. Whisk gently until smooth. Keep warm or at room temperature until serving.
Yield: 2 cups

## Crème Brulée French Toast

1/2 cup (1 stick) unsalted butter
1 cup brown sugar, firmly packed
2 tablespoons corn syrup
4 croissants
5 large eggs
1 1/2 cups half and half cream
1 teaspoon vanilla
2 tablespoons orange flavor liqueur
1/4 teaspoon salt
Powdered sugar

❖ *Grand Marnier is an orange flavored liqueur.*

❖ *Serve warm with warm maple syrup.*

Spray 13 x 9 x 2 inch baking dish with non-stick spray. In a small heavy sauce pan melt butter with brown sugar and corn syrup over moderate heat, stirring until smooth. Pour into prepared baking dish. Slice croissants in half lengthwise. Lay croissants in pan overlapping slightly. In bowl whisk eggs, cream, vanilla, orange flavored liqueur and salt until combined. Pour evenly over croissants. Chill covered overnight in refrigerator. Preheat oven to 350 degrees. Remove French toast mixture from refrigerator. Bring to room temperature. Bake for 40 to 45 minutes at 350 degrees until puffed and edges are pale golden. Dust with powdered sugar. Serve hot.
Yield: 6 servings

## Asparagus, Ham and Gruyère Frittata

12  large eggs
1/4 cup half and half cream
Salt and pepper to taste
2 tablespoons olive oil
1/2 pound asparagus, trimmed ends
1 medium shallot, minced
4 ounces deli ham, 1/4 inch thick
3 ounces Gruyère cheese, cut 1/4 inch cubes

Preheat oven to 425 degrees. In medium size bowl whisk eggs, cream, salt and pepper until well blended. Set aside. Heat oil in 12-inch non-stick oven safe skillet over medium heat until simmering. Add asparagus. Cook, stirring occasionally, until lightly browned and almost tender, about 3 minutes. Add shallot and ham. Cook 2 minutes to soften shallot. Stir Gruyère cheese into eggs. Add egg mixture to skillet and cook. Using spatula to stir and scrape the bottom of the skillet until large curds form and spatula begins to leave wake but eggs are still very wet, about 2 minutes. Shake skillet to evenly distribute eggs and other ingredients. Cook without stirring for 1 to 2 minutes to allow bottom to set. Place skillet in oven and cook for 5 to 7 minutes until eggs are set and top is moist but not runny. Turn on broiler. Place skillet under broiler until top is lightly browned, about 30 seconds. Remove skillet from broiler. Allow to cool on wire rack for 5 minutes. Slide frittata onto a cutting board. Cut into wedges and serve.
Yield: 6 servings

❖ *Sliced fresh tomatoes make an attractive and delicious side dish.*

❖ *Suggested wine pairing - Merlot*

## Kahlua Belgian Waffles

1 cup plus 1 level tablespoon unbleached all-purpose flour
1/2 teaspoon salt
2 tablespoons sugar
2 3/4 teaspoons baking powder
1/2 teaspoon cinnamon
1/8 to 1/4 teaspoon freshly grated nutmeg
2 eggs, room temperature, separated
1/2 cup (1 stick) butter, melted, cooled
2 tablespoons Kahlua
1 1/2 cups milk, less 2 tablespoons at room temperature
1/2 cup pecans, chopped

❖ *Serve waffles with warm syrup, whipped cream and chopped pecans.*

In large bowl sift all dry ingredients, except pecans. In separate bowl combine egg yolks, butter, Kahlua and milk. Whisk milk mixture into dry ingredients. Beat until smooth. Add pecans. Let batter set for 30 minutes. Beat egg whites until stiff, not dry. Fold egg whites gently into batter. Bake according to directions on waffle iron.
Yield: 4 servings

## Egg and Cheese Soufflé

6 eggs
1/2 cup all-purpose flour
1 teaspoon baking powder
1/8 teaspoon salt
1 cup milk
1 cup (8 ounces) ricotta cheese
3 ounces cream cheese, cubed
1 cup (8 ounces) Monterey Jack cheese, cubed
2 tablespoons fresh thyme, chopped
2 tablespoons butter

Preheat oven to 350 degrees. Grease and flour six 8-ounce ramekin dishes. In large bowl beat eggs. Add flour, baking powder, salt and milk. Beat until smooth. Beat in ricotta cheese. Add cream cheese and Monterey Jack cheese. Stirring to blend. Mix in thyme and distribute evenly into ramekins. Dot with butter. Bake for 35 minutes at 350 degrees. Allow casseroles to stand a few minutes before serving.
Yield: 6 servings

## Cherry Vanilla Scones

2 cups all-purpose flour
1/3 cup sugar
1 tablespoon baking powder
1/2 teaspoon salt
1 cup (6 ounces) dried cherries
6 tablespoons cold butter, cut into cubes
3/4 cup heavy cream
2 large egg yolks, slightly beaten
2 teaspoons vanilla

Preheat oven to 400 degrees. In large bowl whisk flour, sugar, baking powder, and salt. Cut butter with pastry cutter until pieces of butter are the size of peas. Add dried cherries. Toss until evenly distributed and coated with flour. In small bowl stir cream and egg yolks until blended. Stir in vanilla. Add to flour mixture. Stir with fork to combine wet and dry ingredients. Gently knead mixture with hands until dry ingredients are absorbed into dough. Gather into soft ball. Do not over knead. Place ball of dough in center of well greased baking sheet. Pat into round 1 inch thick and 7 inches diameter. With sharp knife cut round into 8 wedges. Separate wedges. Brush scones with glaze for scones. Sprinkle with sugar. Place baking sheet on rack in lower third of oven. Bake for 18 to 22 minutes at 400 degrees until deep golden and wooden pick inserted in center comes out clean. Remove from oven and place scones on wire rack to cool for 10 to 15 minutes before serving. Yield: 8 scones

❖ *Dried cranberries can be substituted for the dried cherries.*

❖ *Add egg mixture to flour mixture all at once.*

❖ *Dough will be sticky but benefits from minimal handling.*

❖ *Do not make the round any flatter than 1 inch.*

❖ *For glaze combine 1 large egg, beaten and 1 tablespoon milk. Brush on uncooked scones. Sprinkle with 1 teaspoon sugar.*

## Orange Marmalade Muffins

2 cups all-purpose flour
1/4 cup sugar
1 tablespoon baking powder
1/4 teaspoon salt
1 large egg
1 cup plain yogurt
1/4 cup (1/2 stick) unsalted butter
2 teaspoons vanilla
1/4 cup orange marmalade

❖ *Apricot or pineapple preserves may be substituted for the orange marmalade.*

Preheat oven to 375 degrees. Line muffin cups with liners. In large bowl mix flour, sugar, baking powder and salt to blend. In medium bowl beat eggs, yogurt, butter and vanilla until smooth. Pour flour mixture into egg mixture. Stir just until dry ingredients are moistened. Spoon 1 heaping tablespoon of batter into each lined muffin cup. Spoon 1 teaspoon marmalade into muffin cups on top of batter. Top with 2 more tablespoons of batter in each cup, enough to cover marmalade. Bake for 25 to 30 minutes at 375 degrees until golden brown. Let cool for 5 minutes before removing from cup.
Yield: 8 muffins

## Buttermilk Biscuits

2 cups all-purpose flour
1 teaspoon salt
1/2 teaspoon baking soda
2 1/4 teaspoons baking powder
6 tablespoons cold butter
1 cup buttermilk
1 tablespoon butter, melted

Preheat oven to 450 degrees. In large bowl combine dry ingredients. Cut in butter with pastry cutter. Add buttermilk. Mix with fork. Knead dough lightly on floured surface. Roll dough to 1/2 inch to 3/4 inch thick. Cut with floured biscuit cutter. Place on greased baking sheet. Bake for 9 minutes at 450 degrees. Remove from oven and brush with melted butter. Bake for 1 additional minute.
Yield: 6 biscuits

## Beltane Ranch

The history of the Beltane Ranch starts in 1837 when Juan Alvarado, Mexican governor of Upper California, granted Los Guilicos Rancho to John Wilson and Ramona Carillo de Wilson. About 40 years later the land was purchased for the production of wine and brandy.

The New Orleans style house was built in 1890 by Mary Ellen "Manny" Pleasant and her confidant and banker, Thomas Bell. The house is made completely of redwood. The balcony and porch railing are painted white whereas in New Orleans they would probably be of wrought iron. It has no inside stairs. The home had 10 small rooms about 10 by 12 feet, each opened unto the porch or balcony. Miss Pleasant named the home Beltane after an ancient Celtic festival of Beltane, Ireland held in early May as a celebration of fertility.

Mary Ellen Pleasant was born on a plantation in Georgia, the daughter of slaves. Her mother was a quadroon, born in Santo Domingo, presumably the heiress of a voodoo legacy. Her light skin and the fact that she was educated and freed offered opportunities that seldom occurred in the 1800's. She worked in a store in Nantucket where she met and married a gentleman named Smith who assumed she was white. She became the mistress of his Virginia plantation and his home in Boston.

Mary Ellen arrived in San Francisco in 1852. She was capable and astute in her dealings. She rose to a position of considerable financial and political power during a very colorful period of San Francisco. Financially successful and socially well connected Manny Pleasant managed boarding houses, arranged marriages, operated brothels and numerous other business ventures. It is alleged she was active in the Underground Railway before the Civil War, using the fortune she inherited from her husband to help the escaping slaves.

In 1894, Beltane was deeded to Thomas Bell's widow Teresa Bell. The 1,600 acre ranch later became a turkey ranch and then a working ranch with cattle, horses and sheep.

In the late 60's Rose Mary Wood purchased the property and set about restoring it. The 70 year old house was badly in need of repair. Rose Mary worked on one room at a time. The dividing wall for each of the tiny rooms was removed and the area converted into bedrooms with sitting rooms. Beltane became a bed and breakfast in the late 60's. Today Alexa Wood is the Innkeeper. There are now 5 rooms in the main house and a cottage for guests. Flower gardens surround the home with a large rose garden in front of the house.

## Grandma Royal Coffee Cake

1 cup butter, room temperature
2 cups sugar
2 teaspoons vanilla
2 eggs
2 cups all-purpose flour
2 1/2 teaspoons baking powder
1 teaspoon baking soda
1/2 teaspoon salt
1 1/2 cups sour cream

Preheat oven to 350 degrees. In mixing bowl cream butter and sugar until smooth. Add vanilla and eggs. Beat until fluffy. Sift dry ingredients together. Add to butter mixture. Do not over-mix. Fold in sour cream. Bake in greased baking pan for 20 minutes at 350 degrees. Top with icing and cinnamon.
Yield: 10 to 12 servings

## Beltane Pancakes Royale

❖ *Serve pancakes with a variety of syrups or fruit toppings and whipped cream.*

1 cup all-purpose flour
1/2 teaspoon salt
1/2 teaspoon baking powder
2 tablespoons sugar
2 eggs
1 1/4 cups buttermilk
1/2 teaspoon vanilla
3 1/2 tablespoons butter, melted

Heat griddle to hot. In mixing bowl combine flour, salt, soda and sugar. Separate eggs. Beat whites until stiff. Set aside. In separate bowl combine egg yolks, buttermilk, vanilla and butter. Combine dry ingredients with egg mixture. Mix lightly to leave lumpy. Fold in stiffly beaten egg whites. Drop 1/4 cup mixture on hot griddle for each pancake.
Yield: 6 to 8 pancakes

## Kevin's Korn Muffins

1 1/2 cups all-purpose flour
2/3 cup sugar
1/2 cup corn meal
1 tablespoon baking powder
1/2 teaspoon salt
1 cup buttermilk
2 large eggs
1/3 cup olive oil
3 tablespoons butter, melted
1 cup (8 ounces) creamed corn
1/2 cup (4 ounces) Ortega chilies, diced
1/2 cup green onions, chopped
1/4 cup red bell pepper, diced
1 cup cheese, grated

Preheat oven to 350 degrees. In mixing bowl combine dry ingredients. In separate bowl mix milk, eggs, oil and butter. Combine dry and wet ingredients. Add remaining ingredients. Pour into greased muffin cups. Bake for 18 to 20 minutes at 350 degrees.
Yield: 12 muffins

❖ *This recipe is from Kevin Royal, a chef at the Beltane Ranch.*

❖ *Pepper Jack cheese or cheddar cheese are good additions to this recipe.*

## Mom's Soft Scrambled Eggs

7 eggs
Dash of hot sauce (Tabasco)
Salt and pepper to taste
1 1/2 cups milk
1 tablespoon butter

In mixing bowl beat eggs and hot sauce. In non-stick sauce pan heat milk and butter to hot. Pour eggs into milk in sauce pan. Cook over medium heat. Stir gently with wide spatula until eggs are set.
Yield: 6 servings

❖ *This recipe was developed by Alexa Wood's (Beltane's Ranch owner), mother who first opened the ranch 33 years ago.*

## Sweet Potato Latkes

❖ *To add variety to the latkes try adding either fresh chopped sage, cilantro, cumin or coriander to the batter before frying.*

❖ *Sun-dried tomatoes or artichoke hearts are a delicious addition to the latkes.*

❖ *Suggested wine pairing - Reisling*

3 eggs
1/2 cup half and half cream
1 teaspoon salt
1/2 teaspoon pepper
1 cup all-purpose flour
1 tablespoon garlic, chopped
1/4 cup green onions, chopped
1/4 cup fresh red bell pepper, diced
2 medium size zucchini, grated
2 medium size sweet potatoes, grated
Oil for cooking latkes

Heat griddle to 300 degrees. In mixing bowl combine eggs, cream, salt, pepper and flour. Add garlic, onions, red pepper, zucchini and sweet potatoes to egg mixture. Stir to blend. Drop 1/4 cup mixture on hot grill. Cook, turning once, until golden brown.
Yield: 8 to 12 servings

## Chardonnay Apples

5 Granny Smith apples
1 cup Chardonnay wine
1/2 cup brown sugar
1 teaspoon cinnamon
1/2 teaspoon nutmeg
1/4 teaspoon salt
1 tablespoon butter

Peel, core and slice apples. Place apples in sauté pan. Sauté on medium-high heat until soft and browned. Add wine to pan to deglaze. Add sugar, cinnamon, nutmeg and salt. Simmer to reduce liquid. Remove from heat and add butter.
Yield: 6 to 8 servings

## Raspberry Merlot Sauce

2 quarts fresh raspberries
1 3/4 cups Merlot wine
1 cup brown sugar
1/4 teaspoon allspice
1/4 teaspoon cinnamon
1/8 teaspoon salt

In large sauce pan combine raspberries and wine. Bring to a boil. Reduce heat and simmer for 10 minutes. Strain to remove seeds. Return mixture to heat and simmer. Add allspice, cinnamon and salt. Simmer to reduce by 1/3.
Yield: 4 to 5 cups

❖ *Fresh or frozen raspberries can be used.*

❖ *For a smaller amount cut the recipe in half.*

❖ *Serve sauce with lamb, beef or poultry.*

❖ *Sauce can be served as a topping for baked custard and ice cream.*

## McKenzie's Pancakes

2 tablespoons polenta cornmeal
1 1/2 cups all-purpose flour
1 teaspoon baking soda
1 teaspoon salt
3 eggs
2 cups buttermilk
1/3 cup butter, melted

❖ *Serve pancakes with raspberry syrup.*

Heat griddle to hot. In mixing bowl combine polenta, flour, baking soda and salt. Separate eggs. In a separate bowl beat egg whites until stiff. Mix together egg yolks, buttermilk and melted butter. Add dry ingredients, stirring gently. Fold in beaten egg whites. Do not over mix. Drop by spoonful onto hot griddle.
Yield: 10 to 12 pancakes

## Scrapple Style Polenta

5 cups water
1 teaspoon salt
1 2/3 cups polenta cornmeal
1 pound bulk breakfast sausage, cooked
1 tablespoon dried sage
2 teaspoons freshly ground black pepper
Red pepper flakes to taste

Boil water with salt. Slowly sprinkle in polenta, stirring constantly. Reduce heat and continue stirring until thick. Crumble sausage. Add sausage, sage and peppers to polenta. Pour into buttered loaf pan, cover with plastic wrap. Refrigerate overnight. Loosen gently and turn out onto flat surface. Slice into 8 to 12 slices. Dredge in flour or cornmeal. Cook on well buttered griddle until golden brown.
Yield: 8 to 12 servings

❖ *Adjust seasonings as desired.*

❖ *Add more sage or red pepper flakes if desired.*

❖ *Suggested wine pairing - Gewürztraminer*

## Apricot Muffins

1 3/4 cups all-purpose flour
1/4 cup cornmeal
1 tablespoon baking powder
1/2 teaspoon salt
1 cup sugar
1 1/2 cups dried apricots, diced
1 egg
4 tablespoons butter, melted
1 1/4 cups buttermilk

❖ *The recipe can be cut in half for smaller amount.*

❖ *For a variety in taste substitute apricot nectar for part of the buttermilk.*

❖ *Dried chopped cranberries can replace part of the apricots in this recipe.*

Preheat oven to 350 degrees. In large mixing bowl sift flour, cornmeal, baking powder, salt and sugar together. Add apricots, stir to coat. In separate bowl whisk egg, butter and buttermilk. Add dry ingredients to buttermilk mixture in 3 stages, mixing after each addition. Do not over mix. Pour batter into greased muffin cups. Fill each 3/4 full. Bake for 30 minutes at 350 degrees.
Yield: 12 muffins

*Photo courtesy of Case Ranch Inn*

## Case Ranch Inn

The house on the Case Ranch is a traditional Victorian style farmhouse with an expansive front porch featuring gingerbread trim. It was built by Joseph Walker in 1894 and purchased by James L. Case in 1910. Mr. Case was a Methodist minister in the little town of Forestville, California. He was an active voice in the farm labor movement in the early 1930's. The home became the center of much protest activity during the Great Depression. During this time few people had adequate funds and the church ministers who depended on donations suffered. The Case Ranch was lost in foreclosure in 1941. It was purchased by Mr. Inman from the Analy Bank.

The economy turned around with the event of the war. Mr. Inman was able to pay off the mortgage with the sale of apples and pears from the orchard on the 50 acres of the Ranch. In 1950 the Case Ranch was purchased by Mr. Antipoff and was subdivided over the years with only two acres around the house remaining.

A few years later, Bill and Dorothy Walton bought the ranch with the idea of turning it into a Guest Ranch. They had a summer camp in the Sierras and felt the guest ranch would be successful in Forestville. Bill passed away and left Dorothy with the ranch. A neighbor, George Hill had also lost his wife. and George moved in with Dorothy.

In 1992, Allan Tilton and Diana Van Ry purchased the ranch from Dorothy's estate. I asked Diana when or how she became interested in owning a bed and breakfast. It all started in 1981, when Diana was living in Washington D.C. She took a historical tour of Cape May, New Jersey and fell in love with the beautiful old houses seen on the tour and the idea of owning bed and breakfast started to grow. In 1986 she moved to Forestville, California with Allan who is an engineer.

The two acres they purchased had apple trees, a fig tree, persimmons, plum trees and a deteriorating house. Over the years they planted raspberry bushes and a vegetable garden. They set about restoring the house. They rebuilt the home from the foundation to the roof. In 1999 they moved into a friend's motor home while the inside of the house was completely renovated. Fortunately, the original doors, hardware and floors were able to be saved and refinished. The home was ready to open as a bed and breakfast in 2001.

The Case Ranch Inn has three guest rooms and a luxury guest cottage that was built in 1910 and renovated after opening the Inn in 2002.

I was impressed with the beautiful cherry headboards and bedside stands in the bedrooms and amazed to learn that Allan had made them in his workshop. Diana said, "Allan can fix or make everything".

## Chocolate Buttermilk Cake

4 tablespoons cocoa
1/2 cup butter
1/4 cup vegetable oil
1/2 cup water
2 eggs
2 cups sugar
1 cup buttermilk
1 teaspoon vanilla
2 cups all-purpose flour
1 teaspoon baking soda

❖ *Two 9-inch round cake pans can be used in place of the 9 inch by 12 inch cake pan.*

❖ *Suggested wine pairing - Late Harvest Zinfandel*

Preheat oven to 350 degrees. In sauce pan combine cocoa, butter, oil and water. Bring to a boil. Remove from heat and cool. In mixing bowl beat eggs. Add sugar, buttermilk and vanilla. Add cooled chocolate mixture and beat to blend. Slowly add flour and baking soda. Pour into greased and floured 9 x 12 inch cake pan. Bake for 40 to 45 minutes at 350 degrees until wooden pick inserted in center comes out clean.
Yield: 12 servings

## Chocolate Frosting

4 tablespoons cocoa
1/2 cup butter, softened
4 cups powdered sugar
2 tablespoons milk
1/2 cup nuts, chopped
Water as needed

In mixing bowl slowly mix cocoa and butter. Gradually add powdered sugar, mixing well after each addition. Mix in milk and chopped nuts, adding water to make spreadable consistency.
Yield: Frosting for sides and top of 1 cake

## Sour Cream Pancakes

3/4 cup all-purpose flour
1/2 cup whole wheat pastry flour
1 tablespoon sugar
2 teaspoons baking powder
1 teaspoon baking soda
1/2 teaspoon salt
1 egg
1 cup milk
1/2 cup sour cream
1 1/2 teaspoons vanilla

In a large bowl combine both flours, sugar, baking powder, baking soda and salt. In a medium-size bowl beat the egg. Add milk, sour cream and vanilla. Stir to blend. Add the milk mixture to the dry ingredients. Stir just until combined. Heat a skillet or griddle over medium heat. Brush the surface with butter or oil. For each pancake, ladle 2 to 3 tablespoons batter onto hot skillet. Cook until bubbles start to burst on top. Turn pancake and cook until golden on the other side.

Yield: 12 pancakes, 3 1/2 inch diameter

❖ *Skillet is hot when a drop of water dances across the surface before evaporating.*

❖ *Fresh blueberries may be added to the batter for variety.*

❖ *The batter may have some lumps.*

❖ *If using a non-stick griddle butter or oil is not necessary for the surface*

*Photo courtesy of Case Ranch Inn*

## Persimmon Bread

*❖ Persimmon pulp can be made by pressing persimmon flesh through a food mill.*

*❖ Prepare pulp just before using. It will turn brown if left standing.*

*❖ Persimmon bread can be refrigerated or frozen.*

1 cup persimmon pulp
1 teaspoon baking soda
1 egg
1 cup sugar
1 3/4 cups all-purpose flour
1 teaspoon baking powder
1/8 teaspoon salt
1/2 cup raisins
1/2 teaspoon cinnamon
1/2 teaspoon nutmeg
1/2 cup nuts, chopped

Preheat oven to 350 degrees. Scoop persimmon flesh from the skin of fresh persimmons. Place in blender and blend until smooth. Add baking soda to persimmon pulp. In mixing bowl beat eggs. Add persimmon pulp and sugar. Beat to blend. Add remaining ingredients and mix well. Pour into greased 9 x 5 inch loaf pan. Bake for 45 to 60 minutes at 350 degrees. Allow to cool in pan for approximately 10 minutes.
Yield: 1 loaf

# Blueberry Cobbler

## Blueberry Filling
6 cups fresh or frozen blueberries
1/4 cup all-purpose flour
2 tablespoons sugar
1 teaspoon vanilla
1 tablespoon orange juice
Zest and juice of one lemon

In a large mixing bowl combine blueberries, flour, sugar, vanilla, lemon zest and lemon juice. Place mixture into a large baking dish (approximately 9 x 12 inches).

## Topping for Blueberry Cobbler
1 1/2 cups all-purpose flour
2 tablespoons sugar
1 tablespoon baking powder
1/2 teaspoon salt
1/2 cup unsalted butter, chilled
3/4 cup half and half cream
2 tablespoons sugar

Preheat oven to 375 degrees. In a large bowl combine flour, sugar, baking powder and salt. Cut in the butter until mixture resembles course meal. Lightly toss with the half and half until it forms a soft dough. Drop the dough in tablespoon-size pieces on top of the blueberry mixture until the surface is almost covered. Lightly pat the dough down to evenly distribute the top, but leave spaces for blueberries to show through. Sprinkle with 2 tablespoon sugar. Bake for 40 to 45 minutes at 375 degrees until top is golden and the berries are bubbling.
Yield: 10 to 12 servings

## Lemon Oat Bran Pancakes

3/4 cup all-purpose flour
1/4 cup oat bran
2 teaspoons sugar
1 teaspoon baking powder
1/2 teaspoon baking soda
1/4 teaspoon salt
1 egg
1 1/2 tablespoons butter, melted or vegetable oil
1 tablespoon fresh lemon juice
1 teaspoon zest of lemon
3/4 cup plus 2 tablespoons milk

❖ *1 cup of fresh or frozen blueberries can be added to the batter just before cooking for a delicious variation.*

❖ *Skillet is hot when a drop of water dances across the surface before evaporating.*

❖ *If using a non-stick griddle butter or oil may not be needed.*

In a large bowl combine flour, oat bran, sugar, baking powder, baking soda and salt. In a medium-size bowl beat egg. Whisk in butter or oil, lemon juice, and lemon zest. Add milk and blend well. Add milk mixture to dry ingredients and stir until smooth. Let batter stand for 5 minutes. Heat skillet or griddle over medium-high heat. Brush surface of griddle lightly with butter or oil. Ladle 1/4 cup batter on hot griddle for each pancake. Cook until bubbles start to burst on top. Turn and cook until golden on other side.

Yield: 4 servings of 2 pancakes each

## Persimmon Pudding

1 cup persimmon puree
2 teaspoons baking soda
1 egg, beaten
1/2 cup milk
1 teaspoon lemon juice
1/2 teaspoon vanilla
1 tablespoon butter or margarine, melted
1 cup all-purpose flour
1 cup sugar
1 teaspoon cinnamon
Dash of salt
1/2 cup pecans, chopped
1/2 cup raisins

Preheat oven to 350 degrees. To make persimmon puree, scoop flesh from the skin of fresh persimmons. Whisk in a blender until smooth. Add one teaspoon baking soda to persimmon puree. In a large mixing bowl combine egg, milk, lemon juice, vanilla and butter. In separate bowl sift flour, measure and sift again. Add sugar, cinnamon, salt and remaining 1 teaspoon baking soda. Add to liquid mixture alternately with persimmon puree, blending well after each addition. Mix in pecans and raisins. Pour batter into greased and floured 8-inch square baking pan. Bake at 350 degrees for 55 minutes or until browned. Let cool in pan for 5 minutes. Cut into squares. Serve with lemon sauce.
Yield: 9 servings

❖ *Make the persimmon puree just before using. Puree will turn brown after long standing.*

❖ *Persimmon pudding is best if topped with warm lemon sauce.*

### Lemon Sauce
1/2 cup sugar
2 tablespoons all-purpose flour
1 dash salt
1 cup hot water
2 teaspoons lemon zest
2 tablespoons lemon juice
2 tablespoons butter or margarine

In medium sauce pan combine sugar, flour and salt. Blend in water. Cook over medium heat stirring constantly until mixture boils, is clear and slightly thickened. Add lemon zest, lemon juice and butter. Stir to blend.
Yield: 1 1/2 cups

## Spinach Frittata

2 tablespoons water
1/2 teaspoon dried basil
1/2 teaspoon freshly ground black pepper
1/4 teaspoon salt
1/4 teaspoon dried oregano
8 eggs or 1 carton (16 ounces) egg substitute
1 box (10 ounces) frozen chopped spinach
2 teaspoons butter or olive oil
2 cups sweet onion, thinly sliced
2 cups frozen shredded hash brown potatoes
1 jar (7 ounces) roasted red peppers
3/4 cup crumbled feta cheese

*❖ Vidalia onion is desirable for a type of sweet onion.*

*❖ A freshly roasted red bell pepper can be used in place of the canned roasted red pepper in a jar.*

*❖ If the center of the frittata is not set, turn the oven to bake at 350 degrees and bake until set.*

*❖ Suggested wine pairing - Blanc de Noir Sparkling Wine*

Thaw frozen spinach and squeeze to dry. In a medium-size bowl combine water, basil, black pepper, salt, oregano, eggs, and spinach. Melt butter or heat oil in a 10-inch cast-iron or non-stick skillet over medium heat. Add onions and sauté for 5 minutes. Add potatoes and cook for 9 minutes or until lightly browned, stirring occasionally. Pour egg/spinach mixture over potatoes in skillet. Drain and slice peppers. Arrange pepper slices on top of mixture. Cook 7 minutes on medium heat until set, being careful not to burn the bottom. Sprinkle cheese on top. Preheat broiler. Broil for 5 minutes until cheese is lightly browned and frittata cooked through in the center. Cut into wedges.
Yield: 4 to 6 servings

*Avalon*

English literature of King Arthur's Court describes Avalon as "Country of blessed souls", "Woody isles of Avalon", "Isle of Blest", "Wondrous Avalon", "the fairy isle of Avalon" and "the mists of Avalon". Indeed Avalon is a blissful place that has emerged from tales of old.

Hidden in the redwood forest is this Tudor style home of redwood and reclaimed bricks which to me looked like an English hunting lodge when I first saw it. The narrow, winding driveway with the bridge over the creek did make me feel as if I was coming to a mysterious island in the enchanted forest. Naming the Inn "Avalon" was natural for Hilary and Gary McCalla, who bought the home in 1996 with the intention of creating it into a bed and breakfast.

When I asked Hilary why she wanted to own a bed and breakfast she told an interesting story. Before she was married she was traveling in England with a girl friend. They stayed at a bed and breakfast in London that was run by a charming grandmother. She was very kind to the girls advising them where to go and what to see. She advised them, when they left for the English countryside to stay at a bed and breakfast run by a friend. When they arrived at the recommended bed and breakfast they found a note on the unlocked door telling them to go inside and make themselves at home. The next day they met the innkeeper who was the

most genuinely hospitable and trusting person and truly interested in making them happy and comfortable. On the day the girls were leaving they found another note telling them to just leave the payment on the table or to leave their credit card number. This really had an impact on Hilary and she decided she wanted to be like those two innkeepers, to welcome strangers into her home and make them feel like friends.

The original house was built in 1978 by Bob and Carol Stout who lived in San Francisco and wanted a country home. The architect and the builder fell in love with the project and even finished the two brick light posts at the driveway, even though the Stouts deleted them from the plans. The Stout's lived in the home for only one year and decided it was too far into the country. They moved to Santa Rosa. The house was bought by George and Marybelle Bruss in 1980 as a second home. They never had the opportunity to live in the home. It was a rental property for 16 years.

Hilary and Gary built two guests rooms in the lower level of the main house with private entrances. In keeping with the story of King Arthur's Court, the rooms are named "The Magician's Suite", "The Enchanted Forest" and the third suite in the separate carriage house is named "Guenevere's Tower".

## Hollandaise Sauce

1 cup butter
3 egg yolks
1 teaspoon Dijon-style mustard
1 tablespoon lemon juice

❖ *Hollandaise sauce will keep covered in refrigerator for 1 week.*

❖ *After removing sauce from refrigerator allow it to come to room temperature before reheating.*

❖ *To reheat sauce set container in hot, not boiling, water. Stir until smooth and heated.*

In sauce pan melt butter. Set aside. In food processor or blender blend egg yolks, mustard and lemon juice on high speed, until well blended. With blender running add melted butter a few drops at a time at first, then increase flow to a slow, steady stream.
Yield: 1 1/2 cups

## Caesar Salad Dressing

1 clove garlic, minced
1 tablespoon anchovy paste
6 tablespoons olive oil
1 egg yolk
1 teaspoon salt
1/4 teaspoon dry mustard
Dash black pepper
Dash Worcestershire sauce
3 tablespoons red wine vinegar
Juice of 1/2 lemon (about 2 teaspoons)
3 tablespoons fresh parmesan cheese, grated finely
1 egg yolk, beaten

Combine all ingredients except parmesan cheese. Blend until emulsified. Add cheese. Adjust seasonings to taste.
Yield: 3/4 cup

## Wine Poached Pears

6 large Bosc pears "winter pears"
1 bottle red wine
1 vanilla bean, whole
3 cloves, whole
3 cardamom pods, whole
3 anise seeds, whole
1 stick cinnamon, whole
1/4 cup sugar

Peel pears and cut a slice off the bottom so pears stand straight. Place in sauce pan. Add wine and enough water to cover pears. Add spices and sugar. Cover and simmer the pears until tender. Leave pears in liquid overnight for improved flavor. Remove cold pears with slotted spoon and place on pillow of whipped cream to serve.
Yield: 6 servings.

❖ *Pears can be served with a wine reduction by using the sauce from the pan. Strain out spices before serving.*

❖ *Chocolate sauce drizzled over the pears at serving time is a nice addition.*

❖ *Sugar can be omitted from the wine sauce if desired. However sugar should be added if the wine liquid is to be reduced for serving on the pears.*

## Rhubarb Crisp

3 cups rhubarb, cut into 1-inch pieces
3/4 cup sugar
1 egg, well beaten
1/4 teaspoon mace
1/2 cup butter, softened
1/2 cup brown sugar
1 1/4 cups all-purpose flour

❖ *Topping should be crunchy.*

Preheat oven to 350 degrees. In large mixing bowl combine rhubarb, sugar, egg and mace. Place in 9-inch pie dish. In separate bowl combine butter, brown sugar, and flour. Using a pastry cutter, mix to coarse texture. Spread over rhubarb in pie dish. Bake for 1 hour at 350 degrees. Let cool for 10 minutes before serving. Yield: 6 servings

## Vegetarian Mexican Casserole

❖ *For Vegan vegetarian omit the cheese or substitute with non-dairy cheese.*

❖ *Vegetarian Mexican Casserole is a delicious dish for individuals who do not eat eggs.*

❖ *Use enough tortilla chips so mixture is stiff, but not dry.*

1 can (15 ounces) black beans
1 can (15 ounces) pinto beans
2 to 3 cups tortilla chips, crushed
1 cup tomato salsa
1 teaspoon oregano
1 teaspoon cumin
1 tablespoon dried minced onion
1 1/2 cups cheddar cheese, shredded

Preheat oven to 350 degrees. In mixing bowl combine all ingredients except for 1/2 cup of the cheese. Press mixture into 8-inch square baking dish. Sprinkle with remaining cheese. Bake for 20 minutes at 350 degrees until warmed through. Yield: 6 servings

## Spiced Syrup

1/2 cup sugar
1 tablespoon cornstarch
1/2 teaspoon cinnamon
1/2 teaspoon nutmeg
1/2 teaspoon salt
3 tablespoons lemon juice
1 cup water
1 teaspoon vanilla
2 tablespoons butter

In sauce pan combine sugar and cornstarch. Add cinnamon, nutmeg, salt, lemon juice and water. Bring to boil. Cook until syrup thickens slightly, stirring constantly. Remove from heat. Add vanilla and butter. Stir to blend.
Yield: 1 1/2 cups

❖ *Spiced syrup is good to have on hand. Keep refrigerated.*

## Mexican Egg Soufflé

1 can (7 ounces) green chilies, diced
2 cups cheddar cheese, shredded
2 cups Monterey Jack cheese, shredded
12 eggs
1 teaspoon ground cumin
1 teaspoon flaked cilantro
1/2 teaspoon ground oregano
1/2 teaspoon salt
1/2 teaspoon pepper
1 teaspoon garlic powder

Preheat oven to 350 degrees. Divide chilies into 3 medium 6-inch ramekins that have been sprayed with non-stick spray. Divide cheeses between dishes. In blender whip eggs and remaining ingredients. Divide egg batter among ramekins. Bake for 30 minutes at 350 degrees. Remove from oven and let rest for 5 minutes. Cut soufflés into fourths and serve 2 fourths to each person.
Yield: 6 servings

❖ *Serve with guacamole and salsa. (See recipes on next page).*

❖ *Suggested wine pairings -*
*Gewürztraminer*
*Off-dry Reisling*

### Salsa

1 small yellow onion, peeled, cut into eights
1 cup fresh cilantro
6 ripe Roma tomatoes
1 clove garlic, minced
Juice of 1 lemon (about 3 tablespoons)
1/2 teaspoon salt
1/8 teaspoon pepper

In food processor combine all ingredients and pulse to desired consistency.
Yield: 2 cups

### Guacamole

❖ *If using fresh cilantro increase the amount in the recipe to 1 tablespoon.*

2 ripe avocados
1/2 teaspoon granulated garlic
1/2 teaspoon salt
Dash pepper
1/2 teaspoon cumin
1/2 teaspoon cilantro leaves, dried
1 tablespoon lemon juice
Dollop sour cream

In medium size bowl mash avocados. Add remaining ingredients. Adjust spices to taste.
Yield: 1 cup (depending on size of avocado)

## Raford Inn

$\mathscr{I}$f the Raford Inn could talk it would tell a story of the settling of Sonoma County in California.

Andrew Jackson Peterson's route to California took him from Tennessee to Missouri to Healdsburg, where he secured a Spanish land grant. He married Leidencia Sebring. Together they built the first log cabin in the county. As the family grew in number they acquired more land. Their second son Raford became foreman for the Ranch. During the 1800's Raford Peterson and Charles R. Farmer purchased the Wohler Ranch. It grew to include 1,310 acres.

The mild temperature and appropriate soil made it ideal for growing hops. They were first to grow hops in this area.

The hops business was very labor intensive. At one time over 1,000 laborers were employed on the Ranch to plant, harvest, dry and bale the hops for beer. Most of the workers were Italian immigrants from Fornovolcisco, Italy and San Pellegrinetto, Italy. They would work on the ranch for 2 to 20 years until they accumulated enough money to buy their own piece of land.

In 1920 the ranch was sold to W. C. Chisholm at a value of $350,000. The hop business continued to grow and more Italian immigrants came. W. C. "Billy" died and his wife changed the ranch to a cattle ranch. In the 1940's the hops business suffered a loss brought about by nitrate fertilizer and irrigation causing a mildew mold condition on the hops. At that time the picking of hops had become a mechanical process so fewer laborers were needed.

After Mrs. Chisholm's death, the ranch went to Raford Peterson, the grandson of the first Raford Peterson. He lived on the Ranch until his death when his wife, June Peterson, inherited the property. She stayed on the Ranch until 1980. The Peterson family had lived on the property for 100 years. By this time the size of the ranch had been reduced. Parcels of land had been sold. The first parcel sold was 40 acres to Joe Grace of Santa Rosa, a beer brewer and distributor. The next 500 acres were sold to Fred MacMurry, a Hollywood actor. Then the U.S. Government purchased MacMurray's land plus 90 acres. The government later gave this land to the Santa Rosa College.

Widow June Peterson stayed in the home until 1980 when Beth Foster and Allen Baitinger purchased the home. They set about restoring the beautiful Victorian house. This was a major job but when completed they were able to open a bed and breakfast called The Raford House.

In 2004 Rita Wells and her husband Dane Pitcher bought The Raford House and renamed it the Raford Inn. Dane was most interested in owning a bed and breakfast and has been busy in maintaining the house and grounds. He still holds a job with the City of Santa Rosa, in recreation maintenance. Rita has retired from a career in dental hygiene and now is running the Inn full time.

## Fruit Stuffed French Toast

6 to 8 croissants
1/2 cup cream cheese
3 to 4 bananas
2 to 3 cups strawberries
1/2 cup walnuts, chopped
12 eggs
2 cups milk
1/2 teaspoon vanilla
1 teaspoon baking powder
1/2 teaspoon cinnamon
1/3 cup brown sugar

❖ *Other fresh or frozen fruit may be used in place of strawberries.*

❖ *Nuts are optional.*

❖ *This dish can be baked after assembling rather than refrigerating over night.*

Chop 4 croissants into small squares. Cover bottom of 9 x 13 inch greased pan with croissants. Spread cream cheese over croissants. Cut bananas in thick slices, approximately 1/4 inch thick. Arrange on top of cream cheese. Cut strawberries and scatter over bananas. Sprinkle nuts over fruit. Chop and spread remaining 2 to 4 croissants on top of fruit. In mixing bowl combine eggs, milk, vanilla and baking powder. Beat well. Pour egg mixture over croissants. Sprinkle with cinnamon and brown sugar. Pat mixture to assure croissants are saturated with egg mixture. Refrigerate over night. Remove from refrigerator. Bake for 1 hour at 375 degrees. Yield: 6 servings

## Cranberry Apple Scones

❖ *Cut cold butter into baking mix until coarse meal forms.*

2 1/2 cups baking mix (Bisquick)
3 tablespoons sugar
1/4 cup (1/2 stick) cold butter
1/4 cup dried cranberries
1 medium apple peeled, cored and grated
1/2 cup milk

Preheat oven to 425 degrees. In large bowl combine first five ingredients. Slowly add milk, stirring with a fork until dough holds together. Drop on baking sheet. Bake for 12 minutes at 425 degrees. Yield: 8 scones

## Spinach Feta Pie

1 package (10 ounces) frozen spinach, chopped
1/2 cup mushrooms, sliced
1 teaspoon butter
1/4 cup yellow pepper, chopped
3 green onions, sliced
1/2 cup feta cheese, crumbled

Thaw spinach and squeeze dry. Sauté mushrooms in butter until almost dry. Add pepper and green onion. Sauté 1 to 2 minutes to soften. Add spinach and cheese. Spread evenly in 9-inch pie dish sprayed with non-stick spray.

### Batter
2 eggs
2/3 cup milk
1/4 cup baking mix (Bisquick)
2 dashes hot sauce
1/2 teaspoon salt

Preheat oven to 400 degrees. In mixing bowl beat eggs, milk, baking mix, hot sauce and salt. Pour evenly over filling in pie dish. Gently pat ingredient to cover with batter. Bake for 30 minutes.
Yield: 4 to 5 servings

❖ *More feta cheese can be added, if desired.*

❖ *For variety use different vegetables in pie.*

❖ *Top with a dollop of red bell pepper spread found at specialty food shops.*

## Mediterranean Frittata

8 large eggs
1 1/2 cups artichoke hearts, quartered
1/2 cup black olives, sliced
1/4 teaspoon salt
1/4 teaspoon black pepper
4 to 5 ounces feta cheese, crumbled
2 teaspoons sun-dried tomato pesto
Fresh brochette sauce

❖ *Use fresh cooked or canned artichokes.*

❖ *Suggested wine pairing - Chianti*

Preheat oven to 350 degrees. In mixing bowl beat eggs using fork. Pour into pie dish sprayed with non-stick spray. Sprinkle artichoke hearts, olives and feta cheese on eggs. Dollop pesto over top of eggs. Bake for 40 to 60 minutes at 350 degrees.
Yield: 4 to 6 servings

## Sausage Quiche

1 9-inch pie crust, unbaked
1 cup breakfast sausage, cooked and crumbled
1 cup mushrooms, cooked
2 cups cheese, shredded
1 cup half and half cream
6 eggs
3 dashes hot sauce
Salt and pepper to taste

❖ *Measure sausage and mushrooms after they are cooked.*

❖ *Mexican, cheddar or Monterey Jack are good choices for the cheese in this dish.*

❖ *Hot sauce is optional, if you do not care for spicy hot food omit hot sauce.*

Preheat oven to 375 degrees. In mixing bowl combine cooked sausage, mushrooms, cheese, cream, eggs, hot sauce, salt and pepper. Beat to blend. Pour mixture into pie crust. Bake for 1 hour at 375 degrees, until center is set. Remove from oven and cool on rack for 5 to 10 minutes before serving.
Yield: 4 to 6 servings

## Healthy Harvest Granola

3 cups old fashioned rolled oats
2/3 cup almonds, sliced
1/2 cup unsweetened coconut
1/2 cup hulled green pumpkin seeds
1/2 cup sunflower seeds
2 tablespoons oat bran
2 tablespoons sesame seeds
2 tablespoons wheat germ
1/4 cup butter
1/3 cup honey
1 cup mixed dried fruit
1/2 cup dried bananas

❖ *Granola can be stored in airtight container.*

❖ *Store in cool temperature for up to 2 weeks.*

❖ *Delicious topped with fresh fruit and served with yogurt or small amount of milk.*

Preheat oven to 325 degrees. In large bowl combine dry ingredients, except for dried fruit. In small sauce pan melt butter and honey over low heat stirring constantly. Pour butter mixture over oat mixture. Stir until well combined. Spread granola on jelly roll pan sprayed with non-stick spray. Bake for 15 minutes at 325 degrees. Stir granola half way through baking time. Bake until golden brown. Cool in pan on rack. Stir in dried fruits.
Yield: 7 1/2 cups

## Chili Cheese Puff

❖ Shredded cheddar or Monterey
Jack cheese can be used in place
of Mexican cheese, if desired.

❖ Use a hot sauce such as Tabasco.

❖ Recipe can be doubled to fill
one 10-inch pie dish and serve
8 guests.

❖ Serve Chili Cheese Puff topped
with sour cream, salsa and
guacamole or sliced avocado.

6 eggs
1/4 cup all-purpose flour
1/2 teaspoon baking powder
3/4 cup small curd cottage cheese
1 1/2 cups Mexican cheese, shredded
1 jar (2 ounces) pimentos, diced
1 can (4 ounces) chilies, diced
3 to 4 dashes hot sauce
Salt and pepper to taste

Preheat oven to 350 degrees. In mixing bowl combine all ingredients. Mix well. Pour into 9-inch pie dish. Cover and refrigerate over night. Bake for 50 to 60 minutes at 350 degrees. Remove from oven and let cool on rack for 5 to 10 minutes before serving.
Yield: 6 servings

## Curried Scrambled Eggs

❖ Garnish with chives, green
onions or minced parsley.

❖ For a variation substitute curry
powder with;

  ◆ tablespoon green onion,
  finely minced

  ◆ 1/4 teaspoon dried
  tarragon leaves

  ◆ 1/4 cup smoked salmon,
  in small pieces.

8 eggs
1/3 cup half and half cream
Salt and pepper to taste
1 package (3 ounces) cream cheese
1 tablespoon butter
1/2 teaspoon curry powder
4 English muffins

In mixing bowl beat eggs, cream, salt and pepper. Cube cream cheese. Add to egg mixture. Melt butter in skillet. Add curry powder. Stir and cook to blend. Add egg mixture and cook slowly, gently lifting mixture from sides as eggs set. Cook to desired consistency. Toast English muffin halves. Top with curried eggs.
Yield: 4 servings

## Cowboy Cookies

1 cup butter
1 cup brown sugar
1 cup sugar
2 eggs
1 teaspoon vanilla
2 cups all-purpose flour
1 teaspoon baking soda
1/2 teaspoon salt
1/2 teaspoon baking powder
2 cups rolled oats
1 package (12 ounces) semi-sweet chocolate chips
1/2 cup nuts, chopped

Preheat oven to 350 degrees. In mixing bowl cream butter and sugar. Add eggs and vanilla. In separate bowl combine dry ingredients. Fold into butter mixture. Add chocolate chips, oats and nuts. Mix until combined. Drop by tablespoon onto cookie sheet. Bake for 8 to 12 minutes at 350 degrees.
Yield: 4 dozen

## English Toffee

1 cup sugar
1/2 cup butter
1/4 teaspoon salt
1/4 cup water
1/2 cup blanched almonds, finely ground
3/4 cup chocolate chips, melted
1 cup walnuts, chopped

In heavy kettle combine sugar, butter, salt and water. Bring to boil, stirring frequently until mixture reaches 240 degrees on candy thermometer. Add almonds. Cook and stir to 305 degrees. Remove from heat. When bubbling stops, pour thinly onto well buttered cookie sheet. When cool cover with melted chocolate. Sprinkle with nuts. When firm turn over and repeat chocolate and nuts on other side. When set break into pieces.

❖ *This is a holiday treat that Rita Wells of the Raford Inn has made every Christmas for over 35 years.*

❖ *Store in air tight container up to two weeks, if it lasts that long!*

## Broccoli Salad

4 cups fresh broccoli, finely chopped
1/2 cup sunflower seeds
1/2 cup raisins
1/2 cup cashews, coarsely chopped
1/4 cup green onion, sliced
6 slices bacon, cooked crisp, crumbled

In salad bowl mix all ingredients. Add dressing. Refrigerate 1 hour before serving.
Yield: 4 to 6 servings

## Dressing

3/4 cup mayonnaise
1/3 cup sugar
1/2 tablespoon apple cider vinegar

In small bowl mix all ingredients well.
Yield: 1 cup

❖ *Dried cranberries can be substituted for the raisins.*

❖ *Suggested wine pairing - Sauvignon Blanc*

# Healdsburg Inn on the Plaza

Harmon Heald, a native of Ohio came to California in search of gold. He was unsuccessful in finding gold in mining, however, he made his fortune in land in Northern Sonoma County. By 1852 he had opened a general store next to his cabin. Heald's Store of Heald's Station supplied the travelers, the settlers, squatters and local Native Americans.

Harmon Heald bought large parcels of land at the auction of the Rancho Satoyone, the original Mexican land grant. When official title to the land was straightened out, he laid out eight acres of land and filed a plat map with County Records Office for the town. His fellow citizens named the town Healdsburg. Heald laid out the town around a central park or plaza and donated the plaza to the town. He sold the lots around the plaza for commercial use.

In 1900 Fred A. Kruse retained A. J. Barnett of San Francisco to design a modern commercial building at 112 Matheson Street across from the Plaza. This is the only substantial Victorian commercial building with architectural integrity left on the square. The building is a good example of Italianate style false front with the slanted projecting bays on the upper level. The parapet is nicely detailed with a bracketed cornice with a frieze design. The lower commercial level has been altered loosing some of the significance of the era.

The first occupants of the Kruse building, now the Healdsburg Inn on the Plaza, were the Wells Fargo & Co., Western Union and Vitoussele and Company shoe store. Upstairs was a dentist office, a photography gallery and housekeeping rooms. For the next 100 years the upstairs had rooms and/or apartments for rent. Today the Inn has 12 guest rooms. The Kruse building along with many other brick buildings was severely damaged in the 1906 earthquake. It was rebuilt with some alterations.

In 1973 Larry Wilson started buying up commercial buildings around the Plaza. By 1976 he claimed to own 98 percent of the Plaza stores, including the Kruse building. He declared his plans to tear down everything and build a theme park called the Plaza of Flags. After years of being blocked by the town's residents he sold off the property. Meanwhile, due to lack of commercial business in the Plaza, it became a hangout for the Hells Angels motorcyclists as well as an area full of drugs and violence.

The period of the 1980's was a time of turnaround and the Plaza was cleared. The businesses returned.

In 1980 Chris Decker had a flower shop in the lower level of the old Kruse building. The town folks referred to the building as the Decker building. About this time the upper level was converted into a bed and breakfast, one of the first in Healdsburg. Today the Kruse/Decker building is owned by the Four Sisters Inns and is run as the Healdsburg Inn on the Plaza.

## Roasted Toasted Almonds

2 cups shelled almonds, with skins on
1 1/2 tablespoons olive oil
1/2 tablespoon coarse salt

❖ *The roasted toasted almonds are delicious with a glass of fine sherry or a classic cocktail like a Manhattan.*

Preheat oven to 350 degrees. Fill a 4-quart pot with water and bring to a boil. Boil the almonds for 1 minute. Drain in a colander. Wrap in a towel. Let stand for 5 minutes. Rub off skins using the towel. Place almonds in bowl. Toss with olive oil. Spread on baking sheet. Sprinkle with salt. Bake until golden brown at 350 degrees. Cool and place in airtight container.
Yield: 2 cups

## Cranberry Oatmeal Cookies

1 teaspoon baking soda
1 1/2 cups all-purpose flour
3 cups oatmeal
1 cup dried cranberries
1 cup sweet butter
3/4 cup brown sugar
3/4 cup sugar
1 teaspoon vanilla
1/2 teaspoon salt
2 eggs

❖ *For a variation add 1 cup semi-sweet chocolate chunks to the dough before baking.*

Preheat oven to 350 degrees. Combine soda, flour, oatmeal and cranberries, set aside. Cream butter and sugars until fluffy. Add vanilla and salt. Add eggs one at a time mixing thoroughly after each addition. Add dry ingredients. Refrigerate for 1 hour. Roll dough into 1-inch balls. Bake for 10 to 15 minutes at 350 degrees.
Yield: 6 dozen

## Cheese Blintz

### Filling
2 cups small curd cottage cheese
2 egg yolks
1 tablespoon sugar
1 package (8 ounces) cream cheese, softened

### Batter
1 1/2 cups sour cream
1/2 cup orange juice
6 eggs
1/4 cup sweet butter, softened
1 cup all-purpose flour
1/3 cup sugar
2 teaspoons baking powder
1 teaspoon cinnamon
1/4 teaspoon nutmeg

Preheat oven to 350 degrees. In a mixing bowl beat cottage cheese, egg yolks, sugar and cream cheese. Set aside. Blend batter ingredients. Pour half batter into greased 9 x 13 inch pan. Drop the filing by teaspoonfuls over the batter. Pour the remaining batter over the top. Cover and refrigerate 2 hours. Bake uncovered for 50 to 60 minutes at 350 degrees until golden brown. Cut into squares.
Yield: 12 to 16 blintzes

### Fresh Blueberry Syrup
2 cups fresh blueberries
1/2 cup sugar
1 cinnamon stick
1/4 teaspoon lemon juice

❖ *Serve with blueberry syrup, sour cream and jam.*

❖ *Use fresh or frozen blueberries.*

In sauce pan combine all ingredients. Bring to a boil and cook for 10 minutes. Remove cinnamon stick. Serve warm or chilled.
Yield: 2 cups

## Blueberry Lemon Muffins

1/3 cup sweet butter
1/2 cup sugar
3 tablespoons freshly squeezed lemon juice
1 egg
1 egg yolk
1 1/4 cups all-purpose flour
1/2 teaspoon baking soda
1/4 teaspoon salt
1 teaspoon lemon zest
3/4 cup fresh or frozen blueberries

❖ *For variety substitute orange juice and orange zest in place of lemon juice and lemon zest.*

❖ *Muffins can be frozen.*

Preheat oven to 350 degrees. In mixing bowl cream butter and sugar. Add lemon juice, egg and egg yolk. Mix well. In separate bowl combine flour, baking soda, salt and lemon zest. Gently fold into butter mixture. Spoon batter into greased muffin cups. Arrange blueberries over top before baking. Bake for 15 minutes at 350 degrees.
Yield: 8 muffins

## Pear Clafouti

❖ *Bosc pears are a firm winter pear.*

❖ *Suggested wine pairing - Moscato*

2 Bosc pears
2 large eggs
1 cup cream
1/4 cup all-purpose flour
1/4 cup sugar
Pinch ground nutmeg
Pinch salt

Preheat oven to 400 degrees. Remove stems from pears, core and cut into quarters. Place pears (narrow end to center) in buttered 8-inch quiche pan. Place cream, flour, sugar, nutmeg and salt in food processor. Process until batter is formed. Pour over pears. Bake for 20 minutes at 400 degrees.
Yield: 4 servings

## Hot Salmon Dip

1/2 cup yellow onion, chopped
1/2 cup mushrooms, sliced
1 teaspoon olive oil
1/4 cup green onions sliced
1/2 bunch parsley, chopped
1 1/2 cups cheddar cheese, grated
1 1/2 cup Swiss cheese, grated
1/4 cup water chestnuts, chopped
1 1/2 cups mayonnaise
Pinch cayenne
Salt and pepper to taste
1 can (14.75 ounces) salmon

Preheat oven to 350 degrees. Sauté onions and mushrooms in olive oil until soft. Set aside. In bowl mix remaining ingredients except for salmon. Add onions and mushrooms. Gently stir in salmon. Pour into 8-inch soufflé dish. Bake for 35 to 40 minutes.
Yield: 8 cups

❖ *Red sockeye salmon adds color to this dish.*

❖ *The dip looks very nice served in a round sourdough loaf that has been hollowed out.*

❖ *Serve with crackers or toasted crusty French bread.*

❖ *Suggested wine pairing - Pinot Noir*

## Sunday Eggs

2 cups canned plum tomatoes
1/2 cup shallots, finely chopped
1 teaspoon salt
3 tablespoons sweet butter
2 tablespoons cake flour
1 teaspoon dried basil, crushed
1/2 teaspoon sugar
6 eggs
3/4 cup Fontina cheese, grated

Preheat oven to 350 degrees. In a saucepan combine tomatoes, shallots and salt. Simmer for 15 to 20 minutes on low. Knead butter and flour together. Add to mixture in saucepan. Cook, stirring until thickened. Add basil and sugar. Divide the sauce into 6 small baking dishes or ramekins. Break one egg into each dish over sauce. Sprinkle with Fontina cheese. Bake for 15 minutes until whites of eggs are set.
Yield: 6 servings

❖ *For smaller servings cut the recipe in half.*

❖ *Sunday Eggs are delicious every day of the week.*

## Pasta Salad

2 cups tri-color Rotelli pasta, cooked, cooled
1/2 red bell pepper, chopped
1/2 green bell pepper, chopped
1 cup broccoli, chopped
1/4 cup green onion, chopped
1/2 cup parsley, chopped
1/2 tablespoon dried basil
1/3 cup black olives
1 teaspoon sugar
3 tablespoons olive oil
1 1/2 tablespoons white vinegar
Salt and pepper

❖ *When possible use fresh basil instead of the dried.*

❖ *Seasoned vinegar in place of the plain vinegar adds more flavor to the salad.*

❖ *Garnish salad with sliced tomatoes and parsley.*

❖ *Suggested wine pairing - Dry Rosé*

In large mixing bowl combine all ingredients. Season to taste with salt and pepper. Serve salad cold.
Yield: 6 servings

*Creekside Inn & Resort*

The Creekside Inn and Resort sits right in Pocket Canyon next to the creek that empties into the Russian River. This is a heavily forested area that has been used as a vacation spot for years. In the 1930's it was a great get-away place for workers in the South Bay area. The tourists would come by ferry and train to the Northern Coast of California. The Golden Gate Bridge was finished in 1939 and travel to this area changed to more automobiles. After World War II, travel to the redwood forest along the Russian River increased.

It was about this time that Bill and Margaret Debois developed the property as a campground and resort. They built a family home and rented the upstairs rooms to tourists. They also built platform tents along the creek and rented them. These were able to stand the flooding from the Russian River that occurred almost every year. From 1930 to 1960 cottages were built.

Close by is a 3,000 acre tract called the Bohemian Grove. This is an escape resort for the rich and famous from Hollywood and New York and some politicians from Washington D.C. The area is not open to the public and provides privacy to the stars and public figures. They could party to their hearts content without scrutiny. It was very popular before World War II and still is today.

During the 1950's and 60's groups of young people would gather at the campground and help with outdoor movies and campfires and other activities for the visitors. One of the lumber barons, Cot Armstrong recognized the natural beauty of the area and decided to preserve a piece of land for hiking, biking and enjoyment. He established Armstrong Park adjacent to the Creekside Inn.

Lynn Cresciona lived in Sebastopol and worked in San Francisco and did not enjoy the long commute each day. She decided to find some work that she could do closer to home. In 1980, Lynn and a business partner purchased Creekside Inn. She is now the sole owner. Mark and Craig, her two sons, work with her to run this expanding facility.

I was surprised at how large an area the Creekside Inn and Resort really covers. There are 10 cottages and 6 guest rooms. Lynn is adding 14 more cottages and more guest rooms. All of these will be elevated to prevent flood damage. The outdoor patios are right next to the huge redwoods and creek. It is a lovely setting.

## Creekside Muffins

❖ *Use less sugar in muffins and sprinkle top of unbaked muffins with raw sugar.*

❖ *Raw sugar has larger crystals like sanding sugar.*

❖ *If using dried raisins, cherries or dried cranberries, soak over night in buttermilk. Use this buttermilk in recipe.*

❖ *Muffins can be served warm or cool.*

1 3/4 cups unbleached all-purpose flour
2 teaspoons baking powder
1 teaspoon baking soda
3/4 cup sugar
1 pinch salt
1 cup milk or buttermilk
1/2 cup butter, melted
2 eggs, slightly beaten
1 cup dried fruit

Preheat oven to 375 degrees. In mixing bowl combine flour, baking powder, baking soda, sugar and salt. In separate bowl beat milk, butter and eggs. Add to dry ingredients. Add fruit and mix to blend. Scoop into greased or lined muffin cups. Bake for 15 to 20 minutes at 375 degrees until golden brown.
Yield: 12 muffins

## Simple French Toast

❖ *Save bread crust for croutons or bread crumbs.*

❖ *Serve with real maple syrup, fresh fruit, sautéed apples or pears.*

❖ *Some people like this rich French toast with salt and pepper.*

10 slices sweet French bread, crust removed
10 eggs
2 1/2 cups milk or half and half cream

Slice bread 3/4 inch thick. Place bread in large bowl. In separate bowl beat eggs and milk or cream. Pour over bread. Turn slices in egg mixture to absorb liquid. Refrigerate covered for 8 to 12 hours. Brown each slice lightly on buttered hot grill. Place on lightly oiled baking sheet. Bake for 30 minutes at 350 degrees, until golden brown and puffed. Check that egg is set in center.
Yield: 6 to 10 servings

## Bran Muffins

1 egg
1/3 cup sugar
2 1/2 tablespoons butter
1/3 cup coffee, brewed
1/2 cup plus 2 tablespoons buttermilk
3/4 cup all-purpose flour
3/4 teaspoon baking soda
1 cup wheat bran cereal

Preheat oven to 375 degrees. In mixing bowl beat eggs and sugar. Add coffee and milk. Add flour and baking soda. Mix until blended. Add bran and stir lightly. Let batter stand for 20 minutes. Scoop into greased muffin cups. Bake for 20 minutes at 375 degrees. Cool slightly before removing from muffin cups.
Yield: 8 to 9 muffins

❖ *Canola oil can be used in place of butter. The amount of oil may need to be adjusted depending on the fruit used in the recipe.*

❖ *Fruit can be added to this recipe. Some fruit to select might be raisins, currants, prunes or apples. These will add texture and moisture so less fat may be needed in the recipe.*

❖ *Half whole wheat flour can be substituted for half of the all purpose flour.*

❖ *Prepared batter can be covered and refrigerated for up to 6 weeks.*

## Roasted Red Pepper Strata

2 slices bread, crust removed
2 teaspoons butter
1 tablespoon roasted red bell pepper
1 tablespoon provolone cheese, shredded
12 kernels frozen corn
1 egg
1/3 cup milk

❖ *Recipe can be increased for a larger number of servings*

❖ *White bread seems to work best.*

❖ *Black Forest ham and/or Swiss cheese can be substituted for the provolone cheese, bell pepper and corn in this recipe.*

Preheat oven to 350 degrees. Oil inside of small ramekin with a 1 cup capacity. Butter bread slices on one side. Place 1 slice bread in ramekin, butter side down. Place red pepper, cheese and corn kernels on top of bread in ramekin. Place second slice of bread on top of mixture with buttered side up. In small bowl beat egg and milk. Pour over ingredients in ramekin. Cover. Place in refrigerator overnight or let soak for 4 hours. Place in water bath and bake for 45 minutes at 350 degrees until puffy and golden brown.
Yield: 1 serving

## Waffles

3/4 cup milk
1/2 pinch salt
3 1/4 tablespoons butter
7/8 cup all-purpose flour
4 eggs
1/2 cup milk plus 1/2 cup heavy cream
**Or** 2/3 cup milk with 3/8 cup creme fraiche

In sauce pan heat milk, salt and butter. Bring to a boil. Remove from heat. Add flour all at once. Mix with wooden spoon. Put back on heat. Cook stirring constantly until batter comes way from the sides in a smooth mass and no longer sticks to spoon. Pour into electric mixing bowl. Add eggs 2 at a time, beating on low. Add milk/cream mixture. Spoon into hot waffle iron. Bake until golden brown.
Yield: 3 to 4 servings

❖ *Use an electric beater set at low speed to beat in eggs.*

❖ *Number of waffles will vary depending on size of waffle iron.*

## Baked Frittata

5 to 6 eggs
1/4 cup all-purpose flour
1/2 teaspoon baking powder
1/8 teaspoon salt
1 cup ricotta cheese
1/4 cup olive oil
2 cups provolone cheese, shredded

Preheat oven to 400 degrees. In mixing bowl beat eggs until fluffy. Add flour, baking powder, salt, ricotta cheese, oil and half of the provolone cheese. Pour mixture into greased 8 x 8 inch baking dish. Top with the remaining provolone cheese. Bake for 15 minutes at 400 degrees. Reduce temperature to 350 degrees and bake for 35 to 40 minutes, until lightly brown. Cool and cut into squares.
Yield: 4 to 6 servings

❖ *For interesting taste sensations try adding sautéed onions, potatoes that have been steamed, cubed and browned in some olive oil and/or artichoke hearts either fresh steamed or canned.*

## Green Tea and Pistachio Scones

2 cups all-purpose flour
1/4 cup granulated sugar
2 tablespoons pulverized green tea leaves
1 teaspoon lime zest
1 tablespoon baking powder
5 tablespoons butter, chilled
1/4 cup pistachios
1 cup buttermilk
3 tablespoons confectioner's sugar
1 tablespoon lime juice

❖ *Green tea leaves can be pulverized in the blender.*

❖ *A bench scraper is a good tool to cut wedges of dough.*

Preheat oven to 375 degrees. In food processor mix flour, sugar, green tea, lime zest and baking powder. Cut butter into small pieces and drop in the processor. Process until it is like coarse cornmeal. Drop pistachios in processor and add buttermilk. Pulse until barely mixed. Turn the mixture on to a lightly floured work surface. Quickly form a round ball and transfer to an oiled or parchment covered baking sheet. Flatten the ball until it is less than 1 inch thick and round. Cut with chef's knife in 8 wedges. Bake for 30 minutes at 375 degrees. Remove from oven and cool. Mix confections sugar with lime juice and drizzle over top. Transfer to platter and serve.
Yield:  8 servings

*Village Inn*

The Village Inn in Monte Rio, California turned 100 years old in 2006. Mr. Ludwig was in the timber business cutting redwood for the rebuilding of San Francisco after the 1906 earthquake. He built this "state of the art" home for his family residence. In 1908 he found it was necessary to add on to the building for housing his workers.

The Village Inn was the stage for the movie *Holiday Inn* in 1942 staring Bing Crosby and Fred Astair. The dining room is where Bing sang the song White Christmas that has become a classic. I understand the movie was filmed in the summer so the snow was all fake.

During the 1960's and 1970's this area including the Village Inn became a hang-out for hippies. There was a hippie commune just down the road called Moon Star Ranch. There still are remnants of the campgrounds in the woods.

The Village Inn became a budget housing unit during the 1980's. The building was divided into 28 small rooms. The bathroom was shared. The Rusanowski family owned the Inn for 19 years. In 1986 the lower level was flooded by the Russian River. This happened again in 1995. The county stepped in and ordered them to "get it out of the water"! From 1995 to 1997 the building was completely gutted and renovated.

The restaurant and bar were originally on the lower level. They were moved to the second level as was the new kitchen. Patios for outside dining were added. The dining room and patio have a great view of the river. The lower level was converted into a banquet room and utility rooms.

The 28 little rooms became 4 large guest rooms with private baths in the Inn and the Lodge has 7 guest rooms with private baths.

Mark Belhumeur had a weekend cabin in Monte Rio in the redwoods and would come up from San Francisco often. He thought he would like to open an Italian Restaurant in the area. When a Chinese restaurant came up for sale he considered it but did not act. Two years later it was on the market again. Mark's real estate agent suggested he look at the Village Inn and Restaurant that was also on the market. He and Philip Hampton purchased the property. Mark said he bought a restaurant and got a hotel.

The partnership has worked out well. Mark has a background in food service and hospitality management while Philip is from the high tech world of computers. Mark said, "Nothing stands still when you own an Inn. There is constant maintenance and the need to update". The Inn and restaurant are conscious of the need to conserve natural resources. All the linens are of natural fibers with no dyes. They are hypo-allergenic.

The guests not only have breakfast, but dinner is served Wednesday through Sunday in the dining room. The wine list features 140 different wines, many are gold medal Sonoma County wines of California.

## Savory Cheese Balls

1/2 cup bleu cheese
1/2 cup extra sharp cheddar cheese
1/2 cup goat cheese
1/2 cup cream cheese
Herbs de Provence (to taste)
Zinfandel wine to moisten
Crushed Sweet and Spicy Nut Mixture

❖ *Chef Robert Millington suggests:*
  ◆ *Maytag bleu cheese*
  ◆ *Laura Chenel goat cheese*
  ◆ *Philadelphia cream cheese*
  ◆ *Robert Rue Zinfandel*

Combine all cheeses in food blender. Add Herbs de Provence to taste. Add Zinfandel to moisten mixture to roll-able consistency. Form cheese mixture into balls of bite size portions. Roll bit-size balls in crushed nut mixture to coat evenly.
Yield: approximately 32 cheese balls

## Sweet and Spicy Nut Mix

1/2 cup pecan, halves
1/2 cup cashews, whole
1/2 cup walnuts, halves
1/2 cup hazelnuts, whole
3 tablespoons dark brown sugar
1 1/2 tablespoons maple syrup
1 tablespoon butter, melted
1 1/2 teaspoons kosher salt
3/4 teaspoon cayenne pepper
1/2 teaspoon cinnamon

❖ *Nuts will be shiny and well coated.*

Preheat oven to 350 degrees. Mix nuts on baking sheet. Toast nuts for 10 to 15 minute at 350 degrees. In medium-size bowl mix wet and dry ingredients. Add warm nuts and toss until well coated. Spread mixture on tray. Bake an additional 12 to 20 minutes at 350 degrees. Cool completely. Chop into clusters.
Yield: 2 cups

## Crab and Shrimp Cakes

2 cups crab meat, coarsely broken by hand
2 cups bay shrimp meat, chopped
1 green onion, chopped
1/2 tablespoon fresh parsley, chopped fine
1/4 teaspoon fresh thyme, chopped fine
2 tablespoons mayonnaise
1 1/2 tablespoons Dijon mustard
1 tablespoon fresh lemon juice
1 tablespoon dry white wine
Dash celery salt
Dash white pepper
Dash hot sauce
1/4 cup bread crumbs
2 eggs beaten
Olive oil for frying cakes

❖ *Serve with your favorite aioli and a wedge of lemon.*

❖ *Uncooked cakes may be frozen.*

❖ *Defrost cakes before cooking.*

Mix all ingredients thoroughly and let stand in refrigerator for 1 hour. Form mixture in cakes, approximately 3 1/2 inches in diameter and 1 inch thick. Pan fry cakes until golden brown on each side.
Yield: 6 to 8 servings

❖ *Suggested wine pairing - Buttery-style Chardonnay*

## Black Bean Soup

1 tablespoon vegetable oil
2 medium onions, chopped
2 red bell peppers, chopped
4 celery stocks, chopped
2 carrots, chopped fine
6 cloves garlic, chopped fine
1 Anaheim chili, chopped
1 tablespoon cumin powder
1 tablespoon chili powder
1 pound turtle beans
4 cups chicken stock
1 cup tomato sauce
1/2 cup brandy
Salt and pepper to taste
Sour cream
Green onion, chopped

❖ *More chicken stock may be needed to cover the beans and vegetables.*

❖ *Suggested wine pairings - Dry Sherry Off-dry Reisling*

Heat olive oil in a large pot. Add vegetables and sauté onions, pepper, celery, carrots, garlic and Anaheim chili in hot oil until soft, about 10 minutes. Add spices and beans. Cover with chicken stock to 1/2 inch over ingredients in the pot. Bring to a boil, reduce heat and simmer slowly until beans are tender, about 2 hours. Add brandy, tomato sauce, salt and pepper. Add additional chicken stock if necessary for soup consistency. Simmer for 20 minutes. Garnish with sour cream and chopped green onion.
Yield: 8 to 10 servings

## *Sonoma Coast Villa & Spa*

The Sonoma Coast Villa and Spa started out as the Blue Boar Restaurant back in 1972. It encompassed 240 areas as a farm. It also had 6 guest rooms. The guests could ride the horses over the rolling hills owned by the Blue Boar.

Business was not good for this restaurant in the country and the property was foreclosed in 1980's. A real estate agent in San Francisco had a vision of what the future might be for an inn close to the ocean and not far from San Francisco. He bought the property and restored the buildings. He also added 6 more guest rooms.

In 2005 Johannes Zaehbauer and his wife Ingrid purchased the Inn and named it Sonoma Coast Villa and Spa. Johannes and his wife are both trained professionals in Hotel and Restaurant Management as well as in the Culinary Arts. Johannes was born in Austria and studied in Austria and Switzerland. He met and married Ingrid in Germany. He has worked in the hospitality business in Korea, Hong Kong, China and Europe. He was director of the Food and Beverage at the St. Francis Hotel in San Francisco. When they acquired the Villa they had a clear knowledge of what to expect after operating an Inn in San Diego for 4 years.

The Inn is noted in the brochure as "Tuscany without a passport". The buildings are spread out giving the feeling of open space. They now have 18 rooms all on the first level and each with its own private patio. The red stucco of the outside walls does indeed look like the old villas in Tuscany.

Johannes explained the various types of food service available. The private dinning is for the guests who can order dinner to be served in the dinning room or in the guest's patio if desired. Special events food service might be for weddings, winemaker's dinners, special luncheons or afternoon teas. There is also a special menu known as the Spa Menu for guests desiring specific foods. The morning buffet features homemade pastries, breads, croissants, strudels and rolls fresh from the oven.

The meals are prepared with much of their own produce from their garden. The 60 acre property has apple trees, pear trees and walnut trees. In a few years the orange trees will be producing fruit. The chicken found on the menu is farm raised and most products are locally grown. Johannes uses award winning Cowgirl bleu cheese in his recipes calling for bleu cheese.

There is a separate building housing the Spa. When we walked into the open lounge area I was delighted with the floral fragrance of the room. The small private rooms are equipped for massages of all types, plus facials and scrubs, all to reduce tension.

## Sonoma Organic Rack of Lamb with Mint Sauce

❖ *Prepared Demi-glace can be found in speciality food shops.*

1 rack of lamb
Salt and Pepper,
1 clove fresh garlic minced
Demi-glace

❖ *Suggested wine pairings -*
*Syrah*
*Zinfandel*

Preheat oven to 400 degrees. In hot frying pan cook rack of lamb for 10 minutes on each side. Place pan of lamb in hot oven for 5 minutes for medium rare. Add fresh chopped mint and a little bit of Demi-glace. Stir and serve immediately.
Yield: 2 servings

## Garlic Shrimp

16 medium size fresh shrimp
1 clove garlic, minced
1 teaspoon soya sauce
1 tablespoon fresh lime juice
Salt and pepper as desired

❖ *Serve with fresh vegetables.*

In small bowl combine garlic, soya sauce, lime juice, salt and pepper. Season shrimp with mixture. Grill or broil shrimp for 5 minutes.
Yield: 4 servings

## Baked Brie in Puff Pastry with Mushrooms

1 package (8 ounces) Brie
1 portabella mushroom
Salt and pepper, to taste
1 clove garlic, minced
1 tablespoon soya sauce
1 tablespoon fresh oregano, chopped

❖ *Suggested wine pairing -*
*Pinot Noir*

Preheat oven to 400 degrees. In small bowl combine salt, pepper, garlic, soya sauce and oregano. Coat mushroom with mixture. Saute mushroom for 5 minutes. Cut into small pieces. Wrap Brie and mushroom in puff pastry. Bake for 15 minutes at 400 degrees until golden brown.
Yield: 4 servings

## Grilled Portabella Mushroom

1 fresh whole portabella mushroom
Salt and pepper, to taste
Garlic
Golden oregano
Soya sauce
Aged balsamic vinegar
Virgin olive oil

Place mushroom in marinating pan or dish. Combine remaining ingredients. Taste for desired flavor. Add mixture to mushroom. Marinate for 5 minutes. Grill or cook in a frying pan for 5 minutes, turning once.
Yield: 1 serving

❖ *Makes a wonderful vegetarian dish or side dish with meat, fish or poultry.*

## Bruschette

15 medium pieces of black, green and brunette olives from Turkey
1 red bell pepper, chopped
1 jar (8 ounces) sun-dried tomatoes, chopped
Virgin olive oil, as needed

Mix all ingredients. Serve on toast or thin slices of dark bread. Sprinkle with California walnuts.
Yield: 12 servings as appetizers

## Fresh Wild Salmon with Mango Salsa

8 ounce filet wild salmon
1/2 lime
Salt and pepper and garlic to taste

Juice lime and coat salmon with juice. Add salt, pepper and garlic. Grill salmon in hot pan for 4 minutes on each side. Serve with Mango Salsa.
Yield: 1 serving

### Mango Salsa

1 medium fresh mango, chopped
1 papaya, chopped
1 red bell pepper, chopped
1 green sweet pepper, chopped
1 Roma tomato, chopped
1 clove garlic, minced
1/2 cup Italian parsley, chopped
1/2 cucumber, diced
1/4 cup lemon juice
1/4 cup red onion, chopped
1 teaspoon brown sugar
1 tablespoon olive oil
1/2 teaspoon salt
1/8 teaspoon black pepper
1/4 teaspoon leaf oregano, crushed

Combine all ingredients. Mix. Let set for 2 to 4 hours before using.
Yield: 8 to 10 servings

❖ *Suggested wine pairing - Chenin Blanc*

## North Coast Country Inn

The North Coast Country Inn is located along the Mendocino Coast. The area has a rich history of fur trading, lumbering and ranching. In nearly every dog-hole where a ship could anchor long enough to load timber there was a lumber mill and settlement. The little town of Fish Rock Landing was an active port in the later 1800's. Schooners were loaded with tan bark and railroad ties from a chute on the west point. The protected waters have continued to be a haven for today's commercial fisherman. The town of Fish Rock Landing exists only in a few old photographs and is now known as Anchor Bay. The North Coast Country Inn is located on land that was once a sheep ranch near Anchor Bay.

The original farm house has been replaced with a cluster of rustic redwood buildings and is nestled into a redwood and pine forest. The buildings have rugged shake shingles and fit into the scenery perfectly.

Below the buildings is a lovely country garden with flowers and fruit trees. Some of the original orchard still exists and bears fruit. The garden colors from wildflowers, sea pinks, poppies, lupines, baby breath, azaleas and blue irises vary with the season. The secluded fern covered hillside path under tall pines leads to a hot tub.

The North Coast Country Inn is located with views of the ocean. During the fall and in the spring it is possible to see the whales on their long trip to Baja California and back to Alaska in the spring with their calves. It is also possible to hear the sea lions barking in the distance.

Sandy Walker, the innkeeper, is active in the North Coast Artists' Guild that was founded in 1997 as a part of the Gualala Arts Center. The Inn features the work of the artists in the Breakfast Room. The work of different artists is arranged for a winter exhibit and for a summer exhibit. Their work is for sale in the office and the country antique shop.

## Ham and Cheese Gratin

1 1/2 tablespoons butter
1/4 cup onion, finely chopped
2 celery stalks, finely chopped
3 cups baked ham, cubed
2 teaspoons fresh tarragon, chopped
Ground black pepper
12 hard cooked eggs, peeled
1/2 cup cheddar cheese, shredded

❖ *The secret for the interesting flavor of this dish is the fresh tarragon.*

❖ *It is difficult to cut this recipe in half for a smaller number of servings. Plan to serve Ham and Cheese Gratin when you have a large group present.*

❖ *Ham and Cheese Gratin can be served at breakfast, lunch or for a light supper.*

In small sauce pan melt butter. Add onion and celery. Sauté until soft and translucent, about 3 minutes. Add ham and sauté until heated. Mix in tarragon and season with pepper. Scatter ham mixture over bottom of 13 x 9 inch pan, sprayed with non-stick spray. Set aside.

### Sauce

1/4 cup butter
1/4 cup all-purpose flour
4 cups half and half cream
3 teaspoons fresh tarragon, chopped
1/4 teaspoon dry mustard
Dash cayenne pepper
Dash nutmeg
Ground pepper to taste
8 ounces sharp cheddar cheese, cubed

Preheat oven to 350 degrees. In heavy sauce pan melt butter over medium high heat. Add flour and cook stirring constantly for 2 minutes without browning. Remove from heat. Add half and half. Whisk to prevent lumps. Heat and cook, stirring constantly until thickened, about 2 minutes. Season with tarragon, mustard, nutmeg, cayenne pepper and black pepper. Stir in the cubed cheddar cheese. Cut the hard cooked eggs in half lengthwise. Set 12 halves aside. Coarsely chop the remaining halves and stir into warm sauce. Pour all but 1/2 cup of sauce over ham mixture in baking dish. Nest the reserved egg halves, yolk side up in the sauce, spacing them evenly. Spoon reserved sauce over egg halves. Scatter the shredded cheese over all. Bake for 20 to 30 minutes at 350 degrees until the sauce is bubbling and the surface is golden brown.
Yield: 12 servings

## Spinach and Artichokes in Puff Pastry

1 package (10 ounces) frozen spinach, thawed, chopped
1 can (14 ounces) artichoke hearts, drained, chopped
1/2 cup mayonnaise
1/2 cup parmesan cheese, grated
1 teaspoon garlic powder
1 teaspoon onion powder
1/2 teaspoon pepper
1 package (17 1/4 ounces) frozen puff pastry - 2 sheets

Preheat oven to 400 degrees. Drain spinach well and press between layers of paper towels. In mixing bowl combine spinach, artichoke hearts, mayonnaise, cheese, garlic powder, onion powder and pepper. Thaw puff pastry at room temperature for 30 minutes. Unfold pastry and place on lightly floured surface. Spread one half spinach mixture evenly over pastry sheet, leaving 1/2 inch boarder. Roll up pastry, jellyroll fashion, pressing seal seam. Wrap in heavy-duty plastic wrap. Repeat procedure with remaining pastry and spinach filling. Freeze for 30 minutes. Cut into 1/2 inch thick slices. Place on bake sheet allowing plenty of space between rounds. Bake for 20 minutes at 400 degrees until golden brown.
Yield: 12 rounds per roll

❖ *The second roll can be kept refrigerated for use later.*

❖ *Frozen roll will keep in the freezer for 3 months.*

## Hearty Appetizer Bread Rolls

1 loaf frozen wheat bread dough
Flour for kneading
Dijon mustard optional
Italian seasoning optional
1/4  pound salami, thinly sliced
1/4  pound mortadella, thinly sliced
1/4  pound ham thinly sliced
1/2  pound Swiss cheese, thinly sliced
1/2  pound provolone cheese, thinly sliced
1 egg yolk, beaten and mixed with a little water

❖ *For variety use different kinds of bread dough such as rye, sourdough or multi-grain.*

❖ *In rolling the dough be sure to secure the ends tightly.*

Preheat oven to 375 degrees. Thaw the bread and let it rise, covered in a warm place for 1 hour. Punch down and kneed with a small amount of flour. On a floured surface, roll dough into a rectangle 12 x 16 inches. Spread thin layer of Dijon mustard over the bread dough. Sprinkle Italian seasoning over all. Tear the salami, mortadella and ham into bite-size pieces and sprinkle over the bread. Tear the cheese into pieces and layer over the meat. Starting at the long end roll dough up tightly, jellyroll style. Pinch the ends together tightly and brush with egg mixture. Spray cookie sheet with non-stick vegetable oil. Place bread roll on cookie sheet and let rest for 20 minutes. Bake for 25 to 30 minutes at 375 degrees until golden brown. Let rest a few minutes before slicing. Yield: 12 to 16 slices

# Baked Quesadilla Squares

3 cups cheddar cheese, shredded
3 cups Monterey Jack cheese, shredded
2 cans (7 ounces each) green chilies, diced
6 eggs, beaten
3 cups milk
2 1/4 cups baking mix (Bisquick)
Dash cayenne pepper, to taste
1/2 cup salsa

Preheat oven to 350 degrees. Spray 9 x 13 x 2 inch baking dish with non-stick spray. Sprinkle one third of the cheeses in bottom of baking dish. Top with 1 can chilies. Cover with second third of the cheeses. Top with second can chilies. Sprinkle remaining cheeses on top. In large bowl combine milk, baking mix, eggs and cayenne pepper. Beat until smooth. Carefully pour over chilies. Top with salsa. Bake for 55 to 60 minutes at 350 degrees until golden and puffed. Cut into squares.
Yield: 6 to 8 servings

❖ *Serve with additional toppings as sour cream, salsa and guacamole.*

❖ *These quesadilla squares can be held on a warming tray for hours.*

❖ *Suggested wine pairing - Gewürztraminer*

## Spinach-Mushroom Quiche
## with Cheddar Cheese Crust

**Crust**
1 1/4 cups sharp cheddar cheese, shredded
3/4 cup all-purpose flour
1 teaspoon salt
1/4 teaspoon dry mustard
Dash cayenne pepper
1/4 cup butter, melted

❖ *For variety, use various types of fresh mushrooms.*

❖ *Cooked fresh spinach can be substituted for frozen spinach.*

❖ *Garnish with fresh avocado.*

In mixing bowl combine cheese, flour, salt, dry mustard, cayenne pepper and butter. Firmly press mixture onto bottom and up sides of 9-inch pie dish or quiche pan. Set aside.

**Filling**
1/2 cup onion, chopped
1 1/2 cups fresh mushrooms, sliced
1/4 cup butter, melted
1/4 cup all-purpose flour
1 cup half and half cream
1 package (10 ounces) frozen spinach, chopped, drained
4 eggs, beaten
1 teaspoon salt
1/4 teaspoon nutmeg
Dash white pepper

Preheat oven to 400 degrees.. In skillet sauté onions and mushrooms in butter, until tender. Add flour, stirring until blended. Cook 1 minute stirring constantly. Gradually add cream. Cook over medium heat, stirring constantly until mixture is slightly thickened. Remove from heat. Add spinach, eggs, salt, nutmeg and white pepper. Mix well. Pour mixture into prepared crust. Bake uncovered for 15 minutes at 400 degrees. Reduce temperature to 325 degrees. Bake additional 25 minutes, until set and lightly browned. Remove from oven. Cool on rack for 10 minutes.
Yield: 6 to 8 servings

## Baked Apples with Granola

1 cup raisins
1/2 cup brandy
6 Granny Smith apples
1/2 cup granola
2 tablespoons raw sugar
Cinnamon
2 tablespoons butter
1/2 cup apple juice
1 cup sour cream
1 tablespoon raw sugar

❖ *Sandy suggests Korbel brandy.*

❖ *If raw sugar is not available use white sugar.*

❖ *Mix sour cream and 1 tablespoon raw sugar together. Serve on the side or as a garnish for baked apples.*

Preheat oven to 350 degrees. Cover raisins with brandy. Microwave on high for 1 minute. Let stand to plump. Cut apples in half from stem end and core with melon-baller. Place cut-side up in shallow baking dish. Fill apple cavity with raisins. Drizzle brandy over apples. Crush granola to fine crumbs. Cover raisins with crushed granola. Sprinkle apples with raw sugar and cinnamon. Place butter on top each apple. Pour apple juice in bottom of baking dish. Cover with foil. Bake for 30 minutes at 350 degrees. Uncover and bake additional 30 minutes, until tender.
Yield: 12 servings

## Zucchini-Tomato Quiche
## with Hash Brown Potato Crust

**Potato Crust**
1 package (32 ounces) hash brown potatoes
1/4 cup butter, melted
Salt to taste
Black pepper to taste

❖ *Let quiche stand for 10 minutes after removing from the oven before cutting.*

Preheat oven to 400 degrees. Spray 10 inch quiche pan with non-stick spray. Pour potatoes into quiche pan. Press over bottom to form crust. Brush butter over crust. Sprinkle with salt and pepper. Bake for 25 minutes at 400 degrees, until lightly brown.

❖ *Suggested wine pairing - Sparkling Wine*

**Filling**
1/4 cup onion, chopped
1 to 2 cloves garlic, minced
2 to 3 medium size zucchini, chopped
Basil, oregano and thyme as desired
Salt and white pepper to taste
3 to 4 Roma tomatoes, peeled and seeded
6 extra large eggs, slightly beaten
1/2 cup half and half cream
Seasoned salt to taste
Cayenne pepper to taste
1 cup mozzarella cheese, shredded
2 to 3 tablespoons parmesan cheese, grated

Preheat oven to 325 degrees. In skillet sauté onions for few minutes. Add garlic and zucchini. Season with basil, oregano, thyme. Add salt and white pepper to taste. Peel, seed and chop tomatoes. Wrap in paper towel to remove moisture. In mixing bowl beat eggs and cream. Add seasoning salt and cayenne pepper. Pour zucchini mixture into crust. Pour egg mixture over vegetables. Bake for 25 minutes at 325 degrees. Top with cheeses and tomatoes. Bake additional 10 minutes.
Yield: 6 to 8 servings

## Elk Cove Inn

The The Elk Cove Inn is either in Elk, California or in Greenwood, California. The town actually does have two names. By 1890 Greenwood's population had grown to the point where it needed its own post office. The problem arose when it was discovered that Caleb Greenwood had already received approval for a Greenwood post office in El Dorado County. So Greenwood was forced to choose another name. A herd of Elk in the area provided the inspiration. However as stubborn settlers, the town folks refused to give up its original name. The small town is still officially Greenwood. The Post Office is Elk.

Lorenzo E. White purchased 21 acres with the determination to go into the lumber business. He built a new mill in the cove just south of town. He implemented his vision of a sophisticated system for getting logs to the mill and finished lumber to where it could be graded and stored. He even devised a system for getting the lumber out to schooners for delivery to San Francisco. The company formed a large millpond by damming the creek just below where the Elk Cove Inn now sits. The logs were brought from the forest to flat cars that carried them to the millpond. Log walking pond men, "pole pickers" separated the logs by species and coaxed them into the saw mill at the base of the bluff. By 1890, the mill was producing 100,000 board feet per day.

In 1893 L. E. White built an executive guest house on the bluff overlooking the millpond to accommodate visiting buyers. They were there to negotiate the lumber purchases that helped to build San Francisco back then, and later to rebuild it in 1906 after the earthquake. The house is now the Elk Cove Inn

L. E. White died in 1890 and his son took over the leadership of the business. Unfortunately he died just two years later under somewhat mysterious circumstances. According to local folklore, his wife had been carrying on with a San Francisco attorney, the mills accountant, Frank Drew. Mrs. White was given a medication by the local doctor and instructed to administer it to her ailing husband in very small doses. Word has it that she gave him the whole bottle. He was found dead the next morning. Within a short time Mrs. White married Frank Drew who became president of the company. They took the 1893 guest house as their residence, henceforth called the Drew House. The mill continued to operate for 37 years. It closed in 1930.

Howard Hildrun and Uta Triebeeis became owners of the executive house in the early 1960's. In 1968, they opened the first bed and breakfast on the Mendocino Coast and ran it for 30 years. It became known for it's large German breakfasts. Howard would also entertain guests on Saturday nights by playing his grand piano .

In 1990, Elaine Bryant purchased the property. Elaine was a Southern Belle and the Inn took on a Southern theme. They built the four suites in a large building overlooking the Cove. They sold the propriety to David Lieberman in 2001. The Spa was built in 2003.

## Roasted Baby Beet and Watermelon Salad

4 to 6 baby head lettuce, washed and dried
1 cup watermelon, seeded and diced
1/4 cup pistachio, shelled and roasted
4 kumquats, sliced and seeded
Strawberry Poppy Seed Dressing
6 roasted red beets
6 roasted gold beets
6 roasted baby Chioggia beets
1/4 cup sun-dried golden mulberries
*1/2 cup goat cheese

❖ *Recommended source for goat cheese is Elk Creamery Chèvre.*

❖ *See Strawberry Poppy Seed Dressing on page 186.*

Tear lettuce into bite size pieces. In mixing bowl toss lettuce, watermelon, pistachios, and kumquats. Add salad dressing to lightly coat. Place salad in the center of individual plates. Toss the peeled beets with dressing. Arrange beets around the perimeter of the salad. Top the salad with sun-dried mulberries and goat cheese.
Yield: 6 servings

## Roasted Beets

❖ *A Pyrex pie plate covered with foil makes a good roasting dish.*

❖ *When cool, peel by rubbing beets with a clean dish towel.*

6 baby red beets
6 baby gold beets
6 baby Chioggia beets
2 tablespoons olive oil
1/2 cup orange juice
1 teaspoon fresh thyme leaves
1 teaspoon sea salt
Pinch black pepper

Preheat oven to 350 degrees. Wash and trim beets. Toss with oil, orange juice, thyme, salt and pepper. Place mixture into covered roasting dish. Bake for 30 to 40 minutes at 350 degrees until tender. Cool and peel.
Yield: 18 beets

## Grilled Sea Bass with Dungeness Crab Creole Sauce

2 each 8 ounce boneless bass filets
2 tablespoons Creole spice
2 tablespoons grape seed oil

Preheat broiler/grill to hot. Season each filet with Creole spice and oil. Grill until cooked through, approximately 10 minutes.
Yield: 2 servings

❖ *Suggested wine pairings -*
   *Zinfandel*
   *Syrah*

### Creole Spice
1 tablespoon paprika
1/2 teaspoon sugar
1/2 teaspoon sea salt
1 teaspoon garlic, granulated
1 teaspoon onion powder
1/2 teaspoon smoked paprika
1/2 teaspoon basil, dried
1/4 teaspoon oregano, dried
1/4 teaspoon thyme, dried
1/8 teaspoon celery seed
1/8 teaspoon nutmeg, ground
1/8 teaspoon cayenne pepper
1/8 teaspoon mustard seed, dried, ground

Mix all ingredients in a bowl. Store spice mixture in an airtight jar.
Yield: approximately 4 tablespoons

❖ *See sauce recipe on next page.*

## Crab Creole Sauce

1/4 cup olive oil
1 small onion, diced
1 stalk celery, diced
1/2 green pepper, diced
1 bay leaf
2 tablespoons Creole spice
4 tablespoons garlic, minced
10 Roma tomatoes, peeled, seeded, diced
1/4 cup white wine
1 cup vegetable stock
Salt and black pepper to taste
1 pound Dungeness crab meat

❖ *Sauté to soften but do not brown vegetables.*

In medium sauce pan heat oil and sauté onion, celery and green pepper on medium for 3 minutes to soften. Add remaining ingredients except for crab. Simmer on low for 15 minutes. Add crab and heat.
Yield: 4 to 6 servings

## Elk Cove Inn Signature Cookies

1/2 cup butter
1/2 cup brown sugar
1/2 cup sugar
1 egg
1/2 teaspoon vanilla
1 cup all-purpose flour
1/2 teaspoon baking powder
1/2 teaspoon baking soda
1/2 teaspoon salt
3/4 cup chocolate chips
3/4 cup raisins
3/4 cup walnuts or pecans, chopped
3/4 cup granola mix
1 cup old fashioned rolled oats
1/2 teaspoon orange zest

Preheat oven to 375 degrees. In mixing bowl cream butter and sugars. Add egg and vanilla and mix. Combine flour baking powder, baking soda and salt in bowl. Add to sugar mixture in mixing bowl. Beat to blend. Stir in remaining ingredients. Shape cookie dough into balls slightly larger than a golf ball. Place on ungreased baking sheet. Bake for 8 to 10 minutes at 375 degrees until golden brown.
Yield: 4 dozen

## Strawberry Poppy Seed Dressing

1/2 pint strawberries, washed and trimmed
2 tablespoons champagne vinegar
1/8 teaspoon sea salt
1 tablespoon raw cane sugar
1/4 cup sunflower or almond oil
1 tablespoon poppy seeds

Place berries, vinegar, salt and sugar in a blender. Blend until smooth. Blend on high and slowly drizzle oil into mixture until emulsified. Pour into bowl and stir in poppy seeds.
Yield: 1 1/3 cups

❖ *A tablespoon of water or apple juice may be added to help liquefy the mixture in the blender.*

## Blueberry Cream Cheese Coffeecake

3 cups all-purpose flour
4 teaspoons baking powder
1 teaspoon salt
1 cup sugar
1 teaspoon lemon zest
1 package (8 ounces) cream cheese
1 1/2 cups blueberries, fresh or frozen
3 eggs at room temperature
1/2 cup sour cream at room temperature
1/2 cup butter, melted
2/3 cup milk at room temperature

❖ *Serve the Blueberry Cream Cheese Coffeecake with afternoon tea.*

Preheat oven to 350 degrees. Cut cream cheese into 1/2 inch cubes. In a large bowl combine flour, baking powder, salt, sugar and lemon zest. Add cream cheese and blueberries. Toss to coat with flour mixture. Set aside. In a medium bowl lightly beat eggs and sour cream. Stir in butter and milk. Add egg mixture to flour mixture. Stir until dry ingredients are moistened. Turn into 9 x 12 inch greased baking pan. Smooth the top. Sprinkle with topping. Bake for 50 to 60 minutes at 350 degrees. Let stand for 15 minutes before cutting.
Yield: 8 to 10 servings

### Cinnamon Nut Topping
1/4 cup all-purpose flour
1/3 cup brown sugar, packed
1 teaspoon cinnamon
1/4 cup butter
1/2 cup walnuts, chopped

In a medium size bowl combine flour, brown sugar and cinnamon. Cut in butter until mixture resembles course crumbs. Stir in nuts.
Yield: 1 1/2 cups

## Corn Pudding

1/2 cup butter, melted
1 egg, beaten
1 cup sour cream
1 box (8 ounces) corn bread mix
1 can (16 ounces) whole kernel corn, drained
1 can (16 ounces) cream style corn

Preheat oven to 350 degrees. Melt butter in a 1 quart casserole. In separate bowl add egg and remaining ingredients. Stir to blend. Pour into casserole. Bake for 60 minutes at 350 degrees.
Yield: 8 servings

❖ *Corn Pudding can be assembled ahead of time and refrigerated for 1 to 2 days.*

❖ *Corn Pudding can be frozen before baking.*

## Bread Pudding

1/2 teaspoon vanilla
1 cup half and half, warm
1/4 cup Jack Daniel's bourbon
1/2 stick cold butter, grated
1/2 cup brown sugar
1 teaspoon cinnamon
1/2 teaspoon nutmeg
4 eggs
1/2 cup raisins
6 cups dried bread, cut into 1/2 inch cubes

Preheat oven to 350 degrees. Whisk together vanilla, cream, bourbon, butter, sugar, cinnamon, and nutmeg. Microwave on high for 5 minutes until sugar is dissolved. Cool slightly Add eggs. Beat to blend. Add raisins and bread cubes. Pour into 9 x 12 inch baking dish. Let soak for 20 to 30 minutes. Bake for 25 to 30 minutes at 350 degrees. Serve with Praline Sauce.
Yield: 6 servings

## Praline Sauce

❖ *Reheat in microwave for 2 to 3 minutes before serving.*

3/4 cup packed light brown sugar
1 teaspoon cornstarch
1/2 cup water
2 tablespoons butter, softened
1/2 cup pecans, chopped

Combine sugar and cornstarch in a 4-cup glass measure. Add water and butter. Stir to blend. Microwave on high for 3 minutes until slightly thickened. Stir in pecans.
Yield: 1 1/2 cups

## Orange Scones

1/2 cup butter, room temperature
1 3/4 cups all-purpose flour
1 1/2 teaspoons baking powder
1/2 teaspoon baking soda
1/3 cup sugar
Grated zest of 1 orange
1/3 cup orange juice
1 egg, beaten

Preheat oven to 375 degrees. In a large bowl cut butter into flour until a course meal texture. Add remaining dry ingredients and orange zest. Mix well. Add orange juice and egg. Stir until just mixed. Drop 12 mounds of dough onto greased cookie sheet. Bake for 12 to 15 minutes at 375 degrees until golden brown. Glaze with topping.
Yield: 12 scones

❖ *Recipe can be reduced by half for a smaller number of scones.*

❖ *Pour the glaze on the scones just before serving.*

### Orange Scone Glaze
1/2 cup powdered sugar
1 tablespoon orange juice

In small bowl combine ingredients and mix until smooth.
Yield: 1/2 cup

## Scallop Ceviche

1 cup bay scallops
2 limes, zest and juice
2 tablespoons Rose's lime juice
1 teaspoon sea salt

❖ *Suggested wine pairing -*
*Dry Sparkling Wine*

Combine all ingredients and marinate in refrigerator for 2 to 3 hours, stirring often.
Yield: 1 cup

## Lime Tequila Vinaigrette

3 limes, zest and juice
1/4 cup Rose's lime juice
3 tablespoons water
1/4 cup gold tequila
1 tablespoon cornstarch
1 tablespoon water
1/2 clove garlic minced
1/4 cup cilantro leaves
1/4 cup Agave syrup
1 teaspoon sea salt
1/8 teaspoon black pepper
1/2 cup canola or sunflower oil

❖ *Agave syrup is made from guava and is found in Mexican food markets.*

In a small sauce pan place lime zest, lime juice, 3 tablespoons water and tequila. Bring to a boil. In a small bowl, mix cornstarch and 1 tablespoon cold water until smooth with no lumps. Whisk cornstarch slurry into boiling juices and cook until thickened. Place in a bowl in the refrigerator to cool. When cool place in blender. Add remaining ingredients except the oil and blend on high. Slowly drizzle oil into mixture until completely emulsified.
Yield: approximately 2 cups

## Stevenswood Spa Resort

Little River, California was once called "Big River". In the mid 1800's lumbering was the major industry of the area. Little River was built as a mill town for the vast redwood forests supplying timber for the mill. During the life of the mill over seven billion board feet of lumber was produced and sold.

As the 1800's came to an end so did the lumber business. The sawmill closed, the wharf and chutes deteriorated, the shipping and the weekly steam ship service ended. The area of Little River became part of the State Park System in 1934.

Van Damme State park was named for Charles Van Damme, an early settler of the region. John Van Damme and his wife were a Finnish couple that first settled in this area. The patriarch of the family was born in Ostend, Belgium on May 22, 1832. Van Damme, upon his arrival in Mendocino County, worked in the lumber mill at Little River. In this settlement all of his children were born, including his son, Charles. Charles grew up in the area and became a successful operator of the Richmond-San Rafael Ferry Line. After some years he acquired land along the Redwood Coast. After his death the land became a part of the State Park System.

The Zimmer family owned a piece of land near Little River and adjacent to the Van Damme State Park. For years it was used as a campground for visitors to the North Coast of California. In 1987 the Steven families purchased this parcel of land and built the Stevenswood Lodge. It was designed by famous architect/artist/designer Michael Leventhal. The rustic Inn welcomed visitors until 2004 when Michael Webster and Seth Kelman acquired Stevenswood.

Michael and Seth had been searching for a hospitality adventure for nearly a decade and had visited numerous properties around the world. They set about converting this rustic lodge into a luxury resort and spa. The buildings were gutted and completely rebuilt to have 10 guest suites in the main building. Six of these have ocean views. The full service restaurant was added eight years ago and is open to the public in the evening.

The most recent addition is the 5 star state-of-the-art Indigo Eco Spa. The literature states, "Tranquility, harmony, inspiration and health all in balance".

While reading this information I could not help consider the condition the lumber jacks and mill workers had in the mid 1800's. To them a hot bath once a month would have been a luxury!

# Fancy Baked Egg Scramble

**Mornay Sauce**
1 tablespoon margarine or butter
1 tablespoon all-purpose flour
1/2 teaspoon instant chicken bouillon
3/4 cup milk
1/4 cup Swiss cheese, shredded
2 tablespoons parmesan cheese, grated
1/4 teaspoon white pepper
1/4 teaspoon dry mustard

*❖ Suggested wine pairing - Champagne*

In medium sauce pan melt butter or margarine. Blend in flour and bouillon. Cook, stirring until smooth and bubbly. Gradually add milk. Cook until mixture boils and thickens, stirring constantly. Add Swiss cheese and parmesan cheese. Stir until smooth. Set aside until eggs are done.

**Eggs**
1 1/2 tablespoons butter or margarine
2 tablespoons onion chopped
2 tablespoons green pepper, chopped
1 cup cooked ham, cubed
6 eggs, beaten
1/4 cup canned mushrooms, drained

In large skillet melt butter. Sauté onions and green pepper until tender crisp. Add ham and eggs. Stir just until eggs are set. Fold in mushrooms. Fold scrambled eggs into Mornay sauce. Pour into buttered baking dish. Sprinkle topping over eggs. Bake for 25 to 30 minutes at 350 degrees until light golden brown.
Yield: 4 to 6 servings

**Topping for Fancy Baked Egg Scramble**
1 cup soft bread crumbs
2 tablespoons parmesan cheese, grated
2 tablespoons butter or margarine, melted
1 tablespoon fresh parsley, chopped

*❖ Use a food processor to make soft bread crumbs.*

Combine all ingredients. Stir to blend.

## Chili Relleno Casserole

5 eggs
1/4 cup all-purpose flour
1/2 teaspoon baking powder
Dash garlic salt
1/4 cup butter, melted
1 can (7 ounces) green chilies, diced
1 cup cottage cheese
8 ounces Monterey Jack cheese, shredded

Preheat oven to 400 degrees. In mixing bowl beat eggs. Add flour, baking powder and salt. Stir. Add remaining ingredients. Mix. Pour into baking dish. Bake for 15 minutes at 400 degrees. Reduce heat to 350 degrees and bake an additional 40 minutes. Cool and cut into squares.
Yield: 6 servings

❖ *Top with salsa for variety.*


## Crab Omelets

### Filling
1 tablespoon butter
1 teaspoon garlic, ground
1 roasted red pepper, cut into strips
1 1/2 artichoke hearts, cut thinly
Salt and pepper to taste
2 teaspoons fresh tarragon, chopped
6 ounces lobster cream
8 ounces crab meat
Lemon juice

In skillet heat butter. Add garlic and cook in foaming butter without browning. Add roasted pepper and artichokes. Add salt and pepper. Warm through. Add tarragon and lobster cream. Reduce until thickened. Add crab and warm through. Add lemon juice and adjust seasoning.
Yield: filling for 8 omelets

❖ *Suggested wine pairing -*
*Sparkling Wine*

## Wild Rice Pecan Waffles

1 cup pastry flour
1/4 cup corn meal
1/4 teaspoon salt
2 teaspoons baking powder
1 teaspoon baking soda
1 tablespoon sugar
1 cup toasted pecans, chopped
1 3/4 cups cooked wild rice
2 eggs
1/4 cup vegetable oil (corn oil)
2 cups buttermilk

❖ *Waffle is done when the steam from the waffle iron stops.*

In mixing bowl combine all dry ingredients. Add pecans and cooked rice. In separate bowl beat eggs, oil and buttermilk. Add to dry ingredients. Mix until smooth. Ladle 1/2 cup batter onto hot waffle iron. Bake until golden brown.
Yield: 4 to 6 servings

## Tuscan Baked Scramble

1/2 cup baking mix (Bisquick)
1/4 cup (1/2 stick) butter, melted
4 eggs at room temperature
1 cup cottage cheese
1/2 cup milk, 2 percent
3/4 pound Italian sausage, cooked, crumbled
1/2 cup sun-dried tomatoes, drained well if in oil
1 1/4 cups mozzarella cheese, shredded
Salt and pepper as desired

❖ *Scramble is done if it does not jiggle when the pan is gently shaken.*

Preheat oven to 350 degrees. In electric mixing bowl combine baking mix and melted butter. Mix until smooth. Add eggs one at a time and mix well, scraping sides of bowl often. Add cottage cheese and milk. Mix and set aside. Grease 8-inch baking dish. Add sausage and sun-dried tomatoes to cover bottom of dish. Gently pour egg mixture over sausage and tomatoes in dish. Spread mozzarella cheese over the top. Press slightly into mixture. Bake for 35 minutes at 350 degrees until golden brown. Let cool for 15 minutes before serving.
Yield: 5 to 6 servings

❖ *Top should be golden and all the cheese melted into the egg mixture.*

❖ *Garnish top with crème fraiche and minced parsley on top.*

## Pumpkin Waffles

2 cups pastry flour
1 1/2 teaspoons baking powder
1/2 teaspoon salt
1/4 teaspoon cinnamon
1/4 teaspoon ground ginger
1/4 teaspoon ground cloves
1/4 teaspoon nutmeg
1/2 cup pecans, chopped
1/2 cup vegetable oil (canola)
1 3/4 cups buttermilk
2 eggs
3/4 cup pumpkin

❖ *The pumpkin and spices in this recipe give the waffle a pumpkin pie flavor.*

❖ *After baking sprinkle toasted pecans on the top of the waffle.*

❖ *Serve with caramel syrup.*

In mixing bowl combine flour, baking powder salt and spices. In separate bowl combine buttermilk, eggs and pumpkin. Add to dry ingredients. Stir until smooth. Ladle 1/2 cup batter onto greased hot waffle iron. Remove when steam no longer escapes from hot iron.
Yield: 4 to 6 servings

## Raspberry Chocolate Chip Pancakes

1/4 cup unsalted butter
1/4 cup plus 3 tablespoons milk
1 large egg
1 cup all-purpose flour
2 teaspoons baking powder
1/4 teaspoon salt
1 cup fresh raspberries
1/2 cup semi-sweet chocolate chips

In small sauce pan melt 2 tablespoons butter. Stir in milk. Heat to warm. Whisk in egg. Combine dry ingredients. Add milk mixture. Gently stir in raspberries and chocolate chips. Cook on buttered hot griddle to brown both sides.
Yield: 4 servings

## Crescent Cheesecake Breakfast

2 packages crescent dinner rolls
2 packages (8 ounces each) cream cheese
1 teaspoon vanilla
1/2 cup sugar

Preheat oven to 350 degrees. Butter 9 x 13 inch baking dish. Cover bottom pan with one entire package crescent rolls. Whip cream cheese, vanilla and sugar together. Cover rolls with cream cheese mixture. Place second package rolls over cream cheese filling.

❖ *Pillsbury refrigerated crescent rolls work well for this dish.*

### Topping
1/4 cup butter, melted
1/3 cup sugar
1 teaspoon cinnamon

Melt butter and spread over second layer of rolls. In small bowl mix sugar and cinnamon. Sprinkle over top. Bake for 22 to 25 minutes at 350 degrees.
Yield: 6 to 8 servings

## Swedish Pancakes

❖ *A heavy frying pan can be used in place of a Swedish pancake iron.*

❖ *Heat lingonberries slightly. Serve warm with the Swedish Pancakes.*

❖ *The Kelman way is to serve the pancakes with lemons and powdered sugar.*

❖ *For variety serve pancakes with blueberries, strawberries, applesauce or maple syrup.*

1 1/4 cups all-purpose flour
2 tablespoons sugar
1/2 teaspoon salt
3 eggs
3 cups milk
1/4 cup butter, melted
Vegetable oil for pan coating
1 jar (16 ounces) loganberries or 1 can (16 ounces) jellied whole cranberries

In large mixing bowl sift flour, sugar and salt. In separate bowl beat eggs, milk and butter. Add mixture to dry ingredients. Stir until smooth. Lightly oil surface of pancake pan. Heat Swedish iron pancake pan or griddle. Stir batter just before using. Pour 1 tablespoon batter into each section of hot iron. Tilt pan so batter covers each section completely. When surface of pancake bubbles, turn quickly and brown other side.
Yield: 6 to 8 servings

## *Agate Cove Inn*

The Agate Cove Inn sits on top of a bluff in Mendocino, California overlooking the wild Pacific Ocean. The breakfast room of the main house has windows on three sides so guests can view the waves crashing against the huge boulders. In December, and sometimes in the spring, whales can be seen navigating their passage from Alaska to Baja California and back.

The main building of the Agate Cove Inn was built by Mathias Brinzing, an Austrian immigrant. Back in 1860, Mendocino was a bustling lumber town harvesting the large redwoods. Mathias built his home with the local redwood lumber. Mathias also recognized an opportunity to meet a need of the lumber jacks. After a long day of work at the mill or on the logs the lumber jacks were ready for a beer. He established the first Mendocino Brewery next to the fresh water stream on the land adjacent to his home. This was a successful business for many years.

Some time later, around the turn of the 19th century, a large apple orchard was planted on the bluff by the main house. The weather and land was good for raising fruit trees. Some of these same trees are still producing fruit.

Along about 1970, the Mathias home became a vacation rental home. In 1980, the land and house were sold and then opened as an Inn. Several cottages were added as part of the Inn. Since that time there have been five owners of the property.

Laraine Galloway, the present owner, had not thought about running a bed and breakfast when she first visited Mendocino. She was happy as a teacher in Los Angeles, teaching art and reading for gifted students. Laraine fell in love with this North Coast area. When she discovered the Agate Cove Inn was for sale she decided on a career change. When I visited the Agate Cove Inn, Laraine was still moving her antique furniture, dishes and art work into the Inn to make it more of "her place".

## Agate Cove Scones

❖ *Scones can be frozen before baking. Remove from freezer and bake them at 350 degrees for 45 minutes. These scones seem to come out better if frozen before baking.*

❖ *Select fruit filling :*
- ◆ *1 cup craisins*
- ◆ *1 cup raisins*
- ◆ *1 cup strawberries, diced*
- ◆ *1 cup fresh or frozen blueberries*
- ◆ *1 cup peaches, diced*

❖ *Frozen scones are great to have on hand.*

1 1/2 cups all-purpose flour
1/2 teaspoon baking powder
1/2 cup unsalted butter, softened
3 tablespoons sugar
2 medium eggs
3 tablespoons buttermilk
1 cup fruit filling

Preheat oven to 350 degrees. In bowl mix flour and baking powder. Set aside. In mixing bowl beat butter until creamy. Add sugar, beat until pale and fluffy. Add eggs, one at a time, beating after each addition. Add flour mixture. Stir only to blend. Add buttermilk. Mix only until blended. Sprinkle fruit on top of batter. Fold into batter. Using a scoop, place mounds of dough on ungreased baking sheet, about 2 inches apart. Bake for 30 minutes at 350 degrees until light golden color. Cool on rack.
Yield: 6 scones

## Citrus Cream

❖ *Use as a filling for crepes with addition of strawberries.*

❖ *Citrus cream can be used with pancakes or French toast.*

8 ounces cream cheese, softened to room temperature
2 tablespoons orange zest
1 tablespoon lemon zest
1 tablespoon orange extract
1/2 tablespoon lemon extract
1/2 tablespoon lime juice
1/2 cup sugar
1 cup whipping cream

In mixing bowl blend cream cheese with juices, extracts and zests until cream cheese is completely smooth. Add sugar. Beat to blend. Gradually add cream, beating at medium speed. After cream has been added turn mixer onto highest setting and beat until cream is thoroughly whipped.
Yield: 2 cups

## Chocolate Walnut Cranberry Biscotti

1 cup all-purpose flour
1/2 cup sugar
1/4 teaspoon baking powder
1/4 teaspoon baking soda
1/4 teaspoon salt
1/4 teaspoon cinnamon
1/4 teaspoon ground cloves
2 1/2 tablespoons strong coffee, brewed
2 teaspoons milk
1 small egg
1/2 teaspoon vanilla
1/3 cup walnuts, chopped
1/2 cup plus 2 teaspoons chocolate chips, semi-sweet
1/3 cup dried cranberries

Preheat oven to 350 degrees. Combine dry ingredients. Whisk coffee, milk, egg and vanilla. Add mixture to dry ingredients. Add walnuts, chocolate chips and cranberries to dough. Turn dough onto well floured surface. Roll into 1/2 inch by 3 1/2 inch flat log. Bake on greased floured cookie sheet for 20 to 25 minutes at 350 degrees. Cool. Cut logs into 1/2 inch slices. Reduce oven temperature to 300. Lay slices on cookie sheet and bake for 6 to 8 minutes, on one side only. Cool and serve.
Yield: 16 Biscotti

❖ *For a larger quantity, this recipe can be doubled.*

❖ *Pistachios or almonds can be substituted for the walnuts.*

❖ *Mini semi-sweet chocolate chips work well in this recipe.*

❖ *Chopped dried cherries can be substituted for cranberries.*

❖ *For a more crisp biscotti, bake both sides.*

# Blueberry Bread Pudding

### Batter
2 eggs
1 cup milk
1/4 cup sugar
3/4 teaspoon vanilla
1/2 teaspoon cinnamon
1/8 teaspoon nutmeg
1/2 loaf cinnamon raisin bread

### Filling
6 ounces cream cheese, softened
2 tablespoons sugar
1/3 cup frozen blueberries

### Topping
2 tablespoons frozen blueberries

❖ *Serve pudding warm or cool.*

❖ *Top with blueberry sauce or vanilla sauce.*

❖ *This recipe has been prepared at the Agate Cove Inn using local huckleberries.*

Preheat oven to 325 degrees. In mixing bowl whisk eggs, milk, sugar, vanilla, cinnamon and nutmeg until sugar dissolves. Set aside. Cut bread into 1/2 inch cubes. Add to egg mixture. Mix well. In small bowl beat cream cheese and 2 tablespoons sugar together. Place half bread mixture in bottom of buttered loaf pan. Top with cream cheese mixture and 1/3 cup blueberries. Cover with remaining bread. Sprinkle 2 tablespoon blueberries on top. Bake for 45 minutes at 325 degrees until golden brown. Cool.
Yield: 4 to 6 servings

## Fruit Salad Dressing

2 eggs
1/4 cup sugar
2 teaspoons all-purpose flour
1 cup pineapple juice
1/4 cup lemon juice
1 cup whipped cream

In sauce pan combine eggs, sugar and flour. Beat to blend. Add juices. Cook over medium heat until thickened, stirring constantly. Chill. Before serving fold in whipped cream.
Yield: 2 cups

## Crab Dip

1 cup crab meat
1 cup cream cheese, softened
1/4 teaspoon curry powder
1 tablespoon onion, minced
2 teaspoons lemon juice
1/2 teaspoon horseradish
2 tablespoons almonds, sliced

Preheat oven to 350 degrees. In baking dish mix all ingredients except almonds. Cover top with almonds. Bake for 15 minutes at 350 degrees.
Yield: 2 cups

## Orange Zest Cranberry Sauce

12 ounces fresh cranberries
1/2 cup water
1/4 cup orange juice
1 cup sugar
1/2 tablespoon orange zest
1/2 tablespoon lemon juice

❖ *Orange Zest Cranberry Sauce is delicious served with poultry and with pork.*

❖ *The sauce can be served warm or cold.*

Place cranberries in sauce pan with water and orange juice. Bring to a boil. Cook for 15 minutes until skins burst. Add sugar, orange zest and lemon juice. Simmer berries for 25 to 30 minutes.
Yield: 2 cups

## Lemon Poppy Seed Muffins

1 cup plus 2 tablespoons all-purpose flour
1/4 cup sugar
1/2 teaspoon baking powder
1/4 teaspoon baking soda
1/4 teaspoon salt
1/2 teaspoon poppy seeds
1 egg, beaten
1 teaspoon lemon zest, finely minced
1/2 cup (4 ounces) plain yogurt
2 1/2 tablespoons canola oil
1 teaspoon lemon extract
1/2 teaspoon vanilla

*❖ For a stronger lemon taste use lemon yogurt in place of plain yogurt in the recipe.*

*❖ The Lemon Poppy Seed Muffins freeze well, however do not glaze before freezing.*

Preheat oven to 400 degrees. In mixing bowl combine dry ingredients. In separate bowl combine wet ingredients. Add wet mixture to dry ingredients. Stir to moisten. Scoop into greased muffin cups. Bake for 18 to 20 minutes at 400 degrees. Let rest for 5 minutes before removing from muffin cups. Drizzle with lemon glaze.
Yield: 6 Muffins

## Lemon Glaze

1 tablespoon fresh lemon juice
1/4 cup powdered sugar, sifted
1/4 teaspoon poppy seeds

Combine all ingredients. Stir until smooth and easy to drizzle.
Yield: 1/2 cup

## *Whitegate Inn*

*Y*ou can't miss the Whitegate Inn on Howard Street in Mendocino. It not only has a white gate but also a white picket fence and white oval trellises. The one hundred twenty three year old Victorian home has been restored and maintained to be as magnificent as when it was first built. As was typical of the architecture of the late Victorian period, it is a modified Stick Eastlake effect with New England-like clap boarding on the façade. The exterior is remarkably well preserved considering how close it is to the ocean winds and salty mist.

This beautiful home was built as a doctor's office and as a residence for his family. From 1887 to 1895 it was the local hospital. From 1896 to 1960 it became the health clinic as well as the doctor's office.

In the 1960's and 70's, Mendocino attracted many young people seeking a different lifestyle. The house became a boarding home.

When George and Carol Bectloff bought the home in 1991 they undertook a massive renovating job to restore the home to it original beauty. While remodeling they worked on one room at a time. They were diligent in preserving all the original fixtures that could be saved. Many of the gas fixtures that had been converted to electricity were re-wired. The 15 inch wide ribbon fresco painted around the wall in the parlor is original and worth noting. Some of the door knobs and keys are from the house built in 1883. The crystal chandeliers are also original. George and Carol opened the Whitegate Inn in 1991 and operated the bed and breakfast for 10 years.

In 2002 Richard and Susan Strom purchased the Inn. Richard, a telecommunication attorney and Susan, a high-tech manager set about updating the Inn, while preserving all the original charm.

Richard makes sure the guests are comfortable and happy. Susan who now works with the volunteer fire department is relied upon to consult and advise the activities and changes at the Inn. Kathryn is the steadfast assistant Innkeeper and has been with the Inn for 3 years. Georgina, the housekeeper has been with the Inn for 13 years. Together their efforts assure smooth sailing.

## Whitegate Inn Coffee Cake

1 1/2 cups dark brown sugar
1 cup chopped nuts
2 teaspoons cinnamon
1 cup sugar
1 cup butter, softened
2 eggs
3 cups all-purpose flour
3 teaspoons baking powder
1/2 teaspoon salt
1 cup milk
1/2 cup butter, melted

❖ *Walnuts, pecans or almonds can be used as nuts in this recipe.*

❖ *Chopped black walnuts add an interesting taste to the coffee cake.*

❖ *Cake is done when wooden pick inserted in center comes out clean.*

Preheat oven to 375 degrees. In a small bowl combine brown sugar, nuts and cinnamon. Set aside. In mixing bowl cream sugar and 1 cup butter, until fluffy. Add eggs. Beat well. In separate bowl combine flour, baking powder and salt. Add dry ingredients to creamed sugar mixture. alternately with the milk. Pour half batter into 9 x 13 inch greased cake pan. Sprinkle with half cinnamon sugar nut mixture. Pour remaining batter over cinnamon. Sprinkle with remaining cinnamon mixture. Drizzle 1/2 cup melted butter over batter. Bake for 30 to 40 minutes at 375 degrees. Frost warm cake with Whitegate Glaze.
Yield 12 to 16 servings

### Whitegate Coffee Cake Glaze
1 tablespoon butter, melted
1/2 teaspoon cornstarch
1/2 cup powdered sugar
2 tablespoons hot water

In small bowl mix together all ingredients until smooth. Spread on coffee cake.
Yield: 1/2 cup

## Crab Cakes

2 pounds crab meat
1/4 cup red bell pepper, minced
1/4 cup green bell pepper, minced
1/4 cup yellow bell pepper, minced
1 1/2 stalks celery, minced
1/4 cup sweet red onion, minced
1/2 jalapeno chile, seeded, minced
2 large eggs
1 tablespoon hot sauce
1 1/2 tablespoons Worcestershire sauce
1/2 cup mayonnaise
1/2 to 3/4 cup fine bread crumbs
Peanut oil for frying

Check crab meat for shells. Gently squeeze excess moisture from crab. In large mixing bowl, combine all ingredients except peanut oil. Mix well but lightly. Form into cakes 2 inch diameter by 1/2 inch thick. Pan fry crab cakes on both sides in hot peanut oil. Serve with 1 1/2 to 2 teaspoons of Sherry-Cayenne Mayonnaise. Garnish with lemon wedge.
Yield 8 to 10 servings

❖ *If you prefer a less "hot" mixture reduce the amount of jalapeno and hot sauce.*

❖ *Tabasco sauce is the recommended hot sauce.*

❖ *Recipe can be cut in half for a smaller number of servings.*

❖ *Suggested wine pairing - Chardonnay*

## Sherry-Cayenne Mayonnaise

1 cup mayonnaise
1 teaspoon cayenne pepper
2 tablespoons sherry vinegar

Mix all ingredients together until smooth. Refrigerate until use.
Yield: 1 cup

## Caramel Apple French Toast

1 cup brown sugar
1/2 cup butter
2 tablespoons light corn syrup
1 cup pecans, chopped
12 slices French bread
8 green apples, thinly sliced
6 eggs
1 1/2 cups milk
1 teaspoon vanilla
1/4 teaspoon cinnamon
1/4 teaspoon nutmeg

❖ *Serve with whipped cream.*

❖ *Serve with hot syrup and Canadian bacon.*

❖ *This is a special dish on Sunday morning.*

In sauce pan combine sugar, butter and corn syrup. Cook over medium heat until thickened, stirring constantly. Pour into 9 x 12 inch glass baking dish sprayed with non-stick spray. Sprinkle pecans over syrup. Place a layer of bread on syrup and pecans. Top with sliced apples. In separate bowl beat eggs, milk and vanilla. Pour half of egg mixture over bread in dish. Place second layer of bread on top of apples. Cover with remaining egg mixture. Cover dish. Refrigerate over night. Remove from refrigerator. Sprinkle with cinnamon and nutmeg. Bake for 40 to 50 minutes at 350 degrees.
Yield: 6 to 8 servings

## Avocado Crab Crostini

1 can (6 ounces) crab meat
1/4 cup mayonnaise
1/4 cup sour cream
1/3 cup green onions, chopped
3 tablespoons parmesan cheese, grated
1 jar (4 ounces) pimento, chopped, drained
2 teaspoons fresh lemon zest
1 tablespoon fresh lemon juice
1 teaspoon coarse garlic salt
24 diagonally cut slices French baguette
2 ripe avocados, peeled, seeded and cut into 24 slices

Toast baguette slices to golden brown. In mixing bowl combine crab, mayonnaise, sour cream, onions, cheese, pimento, lemon zest, lemon juice and garlic salt. Top each baguette slice with 3 teaspoons crab mixture. Place avocado slice on top of each. Repeat for all crostini. Refrigerate.
Yield: 24 crostini, 8 servings

❖ *Snack crackers or toasted crackers can be substituted for toasted French baguette.*

❖ *Dip avocado slices in lemon juice to prevent them from browning.*

## Cheese Soufflé

1 cup seasoned croutons
1 cup cheddar cheese, shredded
1 cup Monterey Jack cheese, shredded
1/4 cup green onions, diced
1 package (8 ounces) cream cheese, cubed
14 eggs
2 1/8 cups milk
1/2 teaspoon salt
1/4 teaspoon pepper
1/2 teaspoon prepared mustard
2 dashes hot sauce

Cover bottom of 6 to 8 ramekins generously with seasoned croutons. Top with cheese. Sprinkle with green onions. Place cream cheese cubes over onions. Beat eggs, milk, salt, pepper, mustard and hot sauce together. Pour over ramekins, until almost full. Cover and soak refrigerated over night. Bake for 45 to 55 minutes at 350 degrees, until puffed and golden brown.
Yield: 6 to 8 servings

❖ *Suggested wine pairing - Sparkling Wine*

## Dutch Date Nut Bread

1 1/2 cups boiling water
1 cup dates, chopped
1 1/2 cups sugar
1 egg, beaten
2 1/4 cups all-purpose flour
1/4 teaspoon baking powder
1/2 teaspoon salt
2 teaspoons baking soda
1 cup walnuts, chopped
1 tablespoon shortening, melted
1 teaspoon vanilla

❖ *A loaf of Dutch Date Nut Bread in a festive wrap is a thoughtful gift for friends and relatives.*

❖ *The bread can be frozen. It is good to have the Dutch Date Nut Bread available for special occasions.*

❖ *Different kinds of nuts can be substituted for the walnuts in this recipe.*

❖ *The nuts can be omitted from this recipe, if desired.*

Preheat oven to 350 degrees. Pour boiling water over dates. Let stand for 10 minutes. In mixing bowl add sugar to egg. Beat with a spoon. Sift together dry ingredients. Stir walnuts into dry ingredients. Add date mixture alternately with dry ingredients and nuts to sugar and egg mixture. Add shortening and vanilla. Mix well. Pour into greased and floured 9 x 5 inch loaf pan. Bake for 1 hour at 350 degrees or until wooden toothpick comes out clean. Yield: 1 loaf, 10 to 12 servings

## Chocolate Glazed Pears Ala Whitegate

3 cups water
1/2 cup sugar
1 orange peel twist (2 inches)
6 Bosc pears
6 ounces semi-sweet baking chocolate
2 tablespoons unsalted butter
2 tablespoons orange flavored liqueur

In large sauce pan combine water, sugar and orange peel. Bring to a boil. Pare pears and trim slightly to level bottom. Remove core from blossom end, leaving stem intact. Add pears to poaching liquid. Reduce heat. Cover and simmer gently for 8 to 10 minutes, until tender when pierced with tip of a sharp knife. Turn and baste pears occasionally. Remove pears from liquid. Stand pears on flat dish. Cool. Melt chocolate and butter over very low heat. Add orange flavored liqueur. Dry pears with paper towels. Holding each pear carefully by the stem, spoon chocolate mixture over pear to coat. Place pears in cool place to set chocolate. Arrange pears on 6 individual serving dishes.
Yield: 6 servings

❖ *Grand Marnier is an orange flavored liqueur.*

## Peaches and Cream Cake

**Cake**
2 1/2 cups all-purpose flour
2 1/4 teaspoons baking powder
1/2 teaspoon salt
2 cups sugar
4 eggs
1 cup vegetable oil
1 cup peach schnapps
1 teaspoon vanilla

❖ *Cake is done when it springs back when gently touched or when a wooden pick inserted in center comes out clean.*

❖ *Fresh or canned peaches can be used.*

❖ *Confectionary sugar and powdered sugar are similar and either can be used in this recipe.*

Preheat oven to 350 degrees. Butter and flour two 9-inch layer cake pans. In mixing bowl sift flour, baking powder and salt. In large mixing bowl beat sugar and eggs on medium speed for 30 seconds. Add oil, peach schnapps and vanilla. On low speed blend in dry ingredients. Beat on medium speed for 1 minute. Pour into cake pans. Bake for 35 to 40 minutes at 350 degrees.

**Peaches**
4 cups peaches, peeled, sliced
3 tablespoons sugar
1 tablespoon peach schnapps
In bowl combine ingredients. Stir to blend

**Cream**
1 1/2 cups heavy (whipping) cream
1/4 cup powdered sugar
2 tablespoons peach schnapps

In mixing bowl beat cream to form peaks. Add sugar and peach schnapps.

To assemble, arrange 1 cake layer on plate. Spoon half of whipped cream and half peach mixture on cake. Top with second layer of cake. Spoon remaining whipped cream and peaches on top of cake.
Yield: 12 to 16 servings

## *Joshua Grindle Inn*

Joshua Grindle left Surry, Maine in the middle 1800's to come to the thriving North Coast of California. He, like many others from New England, came to make a fortune in the thriving redwood lumber business. He was employed as a craftsman with the Mendocino Lumber Company for thirty years. He also had interest in the booming San Francisco.

Joshua met and married Alice Hill. Her father gave them a piece of land adjacent to his property on which they could build their home. In 1881 the Grindle's were expecting a baby and hoping for a son. Their son, Aliston Hill was born on January 30, 1882. Unfortunately Alice did not see her new house for she died in childbirth and Joshua was left to raise his son alone.

In June 1883, Joshua married Emma Van Schoick. The house was finally completed in 1883 and the new couple moved in. The date of the home was verified when years later a newspaper dated 1883 was found as the insulation of the kitchen walls. Records show that five years later Emma died in child birth. There is no record of a child so it is assumed the child also died.

Mrs. Eliza Ann Tobin married Joshua in 1890 and Joshua gained two daughters, Elise and Johanna, from Eliza's previous marriage. With the new family, the home became alive with parties and gatherings. Elise's wedding took place in this beautiful two story home.

Joshua Grindle and Fred W. Stickney organized the Mendocino Bank of Commerce in 1905 and Joshua became president of the bank.

In 1917 Joshua sold all his land holdings except the original parcel of land that was given to him by his first wife's father. Eliza died in 1927 and Joshua died in 1928. The home was inherited by Elsie Sutherland, a widowed niece of Mrs. Grindle, who had come from Maine four years previously to take care of the aging Grindle's. She married and lived in the home until 1967 when the home was sold. Joshua's son Aliston was killed in the sinking of the first American submarine in World War I off the coast of Hawaii.

In 1978 the home was converted into a bed and breakfast. It was the first bed and breakfast in Mendocino and must have started a trend because today there are many bed and breakfasts in this little town. The Joshua Grindle Inn has 10 guest rooms in the three buildings on the property.

## Cinnamon Biscuits

2 1/2 cups all-purpose flour
3/4 teaspoon salt
1/4 cup sugar
3 3/4 teaspoons baking powder
3/4 cup butter, chilled
1 1/2 cups half and half cream
1 tablespoon cream for glaze
1 tablespoon cinnamon sugar for topping

Preheat oven to 425 degrees. In mixing bowl combine flour, salt, sugar, and baking powder. Cut cold butter into dry ingredients, until course meal forms. Add half and half cream. Mix. Dough will be lumpy. Scoop onto lightly oiled pan. Brush cream on each biscuit. Sprinkle with cinnamon sugar. Bake for 12 to 15 minutes at 425 degrees, until golden brown.
Yield: 12 to 15 biscuits

## Strawberry Stuffed French Toast

❖ *Recipe can be doubled for 12 servings.*

❖ *French toast can be prepared and refrigerated over night before baking.*

❖ *Serve with warm syrup.*

❖ *Strawberry Stuffed French Toast can be topped with whipped cream, fresh strawberries and garnished with fresh mint.*

1/2 loaf sourdough bread cut into cubes
3/4 cup ricotta cheese
1/2 container (4 ounces) vanilla yogurt
1/3 cup brown sugar
1/2 cup fresh strawberries
6 eggs
1 cup milk
Cinnamon

Preheat oven to 350 degrees. Place half of cubed bread into butter coated or non-stick cooking spray coated 8 x 8 inch glass baking dish. In bowl combine cheese and yogurt to make a thin mixture. Spread mixture over bread. Sprinkle with brown sugar and strawberries. Cover with remaining bread. In large bowl beat eggs and milk. Pour over bread. Sprinkle with cinnamon. Bake for 45 to 60 minutes at 350 degrees. Remove from oven. Cool for 5 minutes before serving.
Yield: 4 to 6 servings

## Eggs Benedict with Smoked Salmon

10 eggs
10 slices rye bread
5/8 pound smoked salmon, cut into thin slices
1 tablespoon fresh parsley, chopped
1 teaspoon capers

In large pot bring 1 quart salted water to a boil. Reduce to simmer. Break eggs into dish and slide egg gently into water. When eggs are cooked to desired consistency, remove from water with slotted spoon. Drain briefly.

**To assemble:**
Toast bread slices and place on warm plates. Top each with slice of smoked salmon and poached egg. Drizzle Lemon Yogurt sauce over each egg. Garnish with parsley and capers.
Yield: 5 servings of 2 eggs each

## Lemon Yogurt Hollandaise

1 cup plain yogurt
2 1/2 teaspoons lemon juice
4 egg yolks
5/8 teaspoon prepared Dijon-style mustard
1/4 teaspoon salt
1/3 teaspoon sugar
1/4 teaspoon black pepper
1 dash hot pepper sauce

In the top of double boiler whisk yogurt, lemon juice, egg yolks, mustard, salt, sugar, pepper and hot pepper sauce. Cook over simmering water for 6 to 8 minutes, stirring until sauce is thick enough to coat back of spoon.
Yield: 1 1/4 cups

❖ *Lemon Yogurt Hollandaise Sauce is also delightful served over grilled asparagus.*

❖ *Using an egg poacher is a convenient way to poach eggs.*

❖ *The lemon flavor of the Hollandaise sauce is a nice complement to the smoked salmon.*

*Photo courtesy of Teri C.*

## Gruyère Cheese Gougeres

1 cup water
7 tablespoons (3 1/2 ounces) unsalted butter
1 tablespoon kosher salt
Pinch sugar
1 1/4 cups all-purpose flour
4 to 5 large eggs
1 1/4 cups gruyère cheese, grated
Freshly ground pepper

❖ *If the ball forms more quickly, continue to cook and stir for a full 2 minutes.*

❖ *Batter will spread while baking.*

❖ *Suggested wine pairing - Extra Dry Champagne*

Preheat oven to 450 degrees. Line baking sheet with parchment paper. In medium sauce pan combine water, butter, salt and sugar. Bring to a boil. Add all the flour at once. Reduce heat to medium. Stir with wooden spoon for 2 minutes, until mixture forms a ball and excess moisture has been evaporated. Transfer dough to mixer bowl fitted with paddle. Beat for 30 seconds at medium speed to cool. Add 4 eggs. Mix until completely combined. Batter will have smooth silky texture. Stop machine. Lift beater to check consistency of batter. Batter should form peaks with tips that fall over. If too stiff, beat in white of remaining egg. Check again and if needed add yolk. Add 3/4 cup gruyère and mix well Add salt and pepper as desired. Fill pastry bag fitted with a 3/8 inch plain pastry tip with batter. Pipe batter into 1 tablespoon mounds on baking sheet, leaving 2 inches between. Sprinkle top with 1/2 teaspoon remaining cheese. Bake for 7 to 8 minutes, at 450 degrees, until puffed and firm. Reduce heat to 350 degrees. Bake an additional 20 to 25 minutes.
Yield: 30 to 35 gougeres

## Yeasted Waffles

2 cups milk
1/2 cup butter
2 1/4 cups all-purpose flour
1 teaspoon salt
2 tablespoons sugar
1 packet (1/2 ounce) dry yeast
3 eggs
2 teaspoons vanilla

In sauce pan heat milk and butter until butter is melted. Cool slightly. In large bowl combine flour, sugar, salt and yeast. Gradually stir warm milk/butter into dry ingredients. Add eggs and vanilla. Mix well. Ladle onto preheated waffle iron. Bake 8 to 10 minutes until crisp on outside.
Yield: 4 to 6 servings

❖ *Hold covered in 175 degree oven until ready to serve.*

❖ *Batter can be prepared a day before serving. Refrigerate over night. Remove from refrigerator in the morning. Punch dough down. Bake on hot waffle iron for 8 to 10 minutes.*

## Sfoof Cake

❖ *Sfoof is a Lebanese dessert. It is rich in the anti-inflammatory spice turmeric. It's flavor resembles a combination of ginger and pepper and is some times described as pungent and bitter. Turmeric is mildly aromatic and lightly orange scented. It is used as an ingredient in many Middle Eastern cuisines.*

2 cups all-purpose flour
1/4 teaspoon salt
1 teaspoon turmeric
1 1/2 tablespoons poppy seeds
1 1/2 teaspoons baking powder
1/2 teaspoon cayenne pepper
1 cup milk
1 cup sugar
1 1/2 cups vegetable oil
1 teaspoon vanilla

Preheat oven to 350 degrees. In large mixing bowl combine flour, salt, turmeric, poppy seeds, baking powder and cayenne pepper. In separate mixing bowl combine milk and sugar. Beat until sugar is dissolved. Add flour mixture and oil to sugar and milk. Mix on medium speed for 5 minutes. Pour into 9-inch round greased cake pan. Bake for 25 to 30 minutes at 350 degrees, until a wooden pick inserted in center comes out clean.

Yield: 6 to 8 servings

## Applesauce Spice Cake

❖ *Whole wheat pastry flour works well in this recipe.*

❖ *If batter is seems dry, add a little more applesauce or a little water.*

1/2 cup molasses
1 cup applesauce
1 teaspoon cinnamon
1/2 teaspoon ground cloves
1 teaspoon baking powder
1/2 teaspoon baking soda
1 3/4 cups all-purpose flour
2 teaspoons ginger, optional

Preheat oven to 350 degrees. In large mixing bowl combine molasses and applesauce. In separate bowl combine remaining ingredients. Stir dry ingredients into applesauce mixture. Mix to blend. Pour batter into 8 x 8 inch non stick baking pan or one that has been coated with non-stick spray. Bake for 30 to 45 minutes at 350 degrees until wooden pick when inserted in center comes out clean. Cool on wire rack.

Yield: 6 to 8 servings

## Apple Stuffed Crepes

### Crepe Batter

1 cup all-purpose flour
1 2/3 cups milk
1 egg, slightly beaten
1 tablespoon butter, melted
Pinch salt

In mixing bowl combine all ingredients. Beat until smooth. Heat crepe pan or 7 to 8 inch skillet over medium high heat. Grease pan lightly. Pour 3 tablespoons batter into hot pan, tilting pan to spread evenly. When crepe is lightly brown, turn to brown other side. Remove from pan and keep warm. Repeat for additional crepes.

❖ *Batter for the crepe can be prepared the day before serving.*

## Braised Apples

4 apples, peeled, cored and chopped
1 cup apple or cranberry juice
1 tablespoon cornstarch
3 tablespoons brown sugar
3 tablespoons butter
2 teaspoons cinnamon
1/2 teaspoon ground cloves
1/2 teaspoon nutmeg

*❖ One tablespoon baking spice can be substituted for the cinnamon, cloves and nutmeg.*

In small bowl dissolve cornstarch in 2 tablespoon juice. Set aside. In sauce pan combine apples and remaining ingredients. Cook until apples are soft. Add cornstarch mixture. Cook and stir until thickened.

## Cinnamon Cheese Mixture

1 cup ricotta cheese
1 cup cottage cheese
3 tablespoons cinnamon sugar
1/3 cup dried cherries or dried cranberries
1/3 cup granola

*❖ Crepes can be served with whipped cream and a sprinkling of walnuts and dried cherries or dried cranberries.*

In bowl combine all ingredients. Layer crepes, apples and cheese alternating layers,. Bake for 30 minutes at 350 degrees. Cut layered crepes into wedges to serve.
Yield: 6 servings

## The Weller House Inn

The Fort Bragg area in Northern California was once the homeland for the Pomo tribe of North American Indians. They were hunter-gathers who lived close to the land and the sea. In 1856 the Bureau of Indian Affairs established the Mendocino reservation. The following year a military post was established for the purpose of maintaining order on the reservation. It was named Fort Bragg in honor of Captain Braxton Bragg, who later became a General in the army of the Confederacy. The garrison remained until October of 1864 when it was loaded aboard the steamer "Pomona" and evacuated the Mendocino County's first military post. The Mendocino Indian Reservation was discontinued in 1886 and the land was opened for sale at $1.25 per acre to settlers.

Horace Weller was one of the early settlers in Fort Bragg. To meet the needs of this fast growing community, he founded the first bank in Fort Bragg. Horace and his wife built a Victorian style home in central Fort Bragg in 1886. Ten years later Mr. Weller added a third level consisting mainly of a grand ballroom, beautifully paneled in the local redwood. The town folks were fascinated to see a grand piano lowered into the ballroom by a crane before the roof was in place.

Over the past century, the Weller House has changed hands several times. Fortunately the integrity of the Victorian home was not destroyed.

In 1997, Ted and Eva Kidwell were browsing among real estate offices in Mendocino County looking for a bed and breakfast that might be for sale. They came upon the Weller House that was unoccupied and slowly falling into disrepair. They felt it had potential for becoming a bed and breakfast. They purchased the home, moved from Marin County and began the extensive renovations.

Ted's background allowed him to supervise the reconstruction as well as do a large portion of the work. Eva was responsible for collecting and restoring many of the valuable antiques now in the home. The renovation included building the eight guests rooms, the addition of ten private bathrooms, radiant floor heating in all rooms and decoration of the rooms in authentic Victorian style from wallpaper to furnishings.

A unique feature of the Weller House Inn is the reconstructed city water tower adjacent to the house. When built in the early 1900's it was the tallest building in Fort Bragg. It is again the tallest building, however today, it holds two guests suites instead of the city water.

## Open-Face Soufflé Sandwich

1/2 sandwich size English muffin, toasted
1/2 teaspoon butter
1 slice honey cured ham
1/2 cup mozzarella cheese, shredded
1 egg, separated
Salt and pepper to taste

❖ *Egg will puff when baked. Serve immediately.*

Preheat oven to 350 degrees. Place toasted English muffin on baking pan lightly coat with butter. Place ham on top of muffin. Set aside. Whip egg white until very stiff. Gently add egg yolk and cheese to egg white. Add salt and pepper. Place egg mixture on top of ham. Bake for 15 to 20 minutes at 350 degrees, until golden brown.
Yield: 1 serving

## Stuffed French Toast

1/2 loaf French bread
1 small package (3 ounces) cream cheese
1/2 cup cottage cheese
2 tablespoons fruit jam
1 cup milk
2 eggs
1/4 cup sugar
1/8 teaspoon nutmeg
1/8 teaspoon ground ginger
1/2 teaspoon vanilla

❖ *The Stuffed French Toast is delicious served with blueberry sauce and sausage.*

Cut bread into thick slices. Make a slit through the center of each slice for a pocket. In bowl combine cream cheese and cottage cheese. Add jam. Fill each pocket with cheese mixture. In mixing bowl combine milk, eggs and flavorings. Pour over bread to soak. In skillet fry each slice over medium heat. Turn to brown second side.
Yield: 4 to 6 servings

## Honey Coconut Granola

7 1/2 cups old fashioned oatmeal
1/2 cup walnuts, chopped
1/2 cup wheat germ
1/2 cup sunflower seeds
1 cup flaked coconut
1/2 cup butter or margarine
1/2 cup brown sugar
1/2 cup honey
1/4 cup vegetable oil
1/2 tablespoon vanilla
1/2 tablespoon maple syrup
1/4 teaspoon salt
1/2 cup raisins

Preheat oven to 275 degrees. In large bowl combine oatmeal, walnuts, wheat germ, sunflower seeds and coconut. In sauce pan heat butter, brown sugar, honey, oil, flavorings and salt until hot and well mixed. Pour warm mixture over oatmeal mixture in bowl. Stir to coat evenly. Pour onto greased baking pans. Bake for 60 to 70 minutes at 275 degrees. Stir occasionally.
Yield: 10 cups

❖ *Store granola in an airtight container.*

❖ *This is a popular breakfast item but is good at any time of day.*

## Eva's Shredded Apple Pie

1 unbaked 9-inch pastry crust
1 egg white
1/2 cup butter or margarine
1 cup sugar
2 eggs
4 to 5 apples, shredded
1 lemon peel, shredded

❖ *The shredded apples will resemble shredded cheese.*

❖ *Serve with whipped cream or ice cream.*

Preheat oven to 325 degrees Brush pie crust with egg white. Melt butter and whip until light and airy. Add eggs one at a time. Beat. Add apples and lemon peel. Pour into crust. Bake for 25 to 35 minutes at 325 degrees.
Yield: 6 servings

## Tomato Polenta and Goat Cheese Tart

1 cup yellow cornmeal
4 teaspoons olive oil, divided
1/2 teaspoon salt
2 cloves garlic, minced
2 1/2 cups water
1 cup tomato juice
Vegetable cooking spray
1/3 cup non-fat cream cheese
1/2 cup goat cheese
1 egg
1 cup zucchini, thinly sliced
1 cup yellow squash, thinly sliced
1 tablespoon dried thyme leaves, crushed
1 tablespoon parmesan cheese, grated

❖ *The tart is a nice alternative to quiche.*

❖ *Serve the polenta tomato tart as a vegetarian dish.*

❖ *Suggested wine pairing - Fumé Blanc*

Preheat oven to 400 degrees. Place cornmeal, 3 teaspoons oil, salt and garlic in large sauce pan. Gradually add water and tomato juice, stirring constantly with wire whisk. Bring to a boil. Reduce heat to medium. Cook uncovered for 10 minutes, stirring frequently. Spread mixture in bottom of spring form tart pan, coated with vegetable spray. In food processor blend cream cheese, goat cheese and egg, until smooth. Spread cream cheese mixture over polenta. Arrange zucchini and squash alternately over cream cheese mixture. Brush remaining oil over vegetables. Sprinkle thyme and parmesan over tart. Bake for 15 minutes at 400 degrees. Broil for 1 minute to slightly brown top.
Yield: 6 servings

## Asparagus Quiche

1 10-inch pastry shell, unbaked
1 pound fresh asparagus
1 teaspoon salt
1 egg white
2 cups Swiss cheese, shredded
10 strips bacon, cooked and crumbled
4 eggs
1 1/2 cups half and half cream
1/4 teaspoon nutmeg, ground
1/4 teaspoon salt
1 pinch pepper
Cherry tomatoes, halved

❖ *Suggested wine pairing -*
*Pinot Noir*

Preheat oven to 400 degrees. Cut 8 asparagus spears 4 inches long for garnish. Cut remaining asparagus into 1/2 inch pieces. In large saucepan boil 1 quart of water. Add all asparagus and salt. Return to boil. Reduce heat, cover and simmer for 5 minutes. Drain and rinse asparagus. Brush bottom of pastry shell with egg white. In a bowl combine 1/2 inch asparagus, Swiss cheese and bacon. Mix gently. Place in the pastry shell. In a separate bowl beat eggs, cream and nutmeg, salt and pepper until smooth. Pour in pastry shell. Bake uncovered for 35 to 40 minutes at 400 degrees until knife inserted in center comes out clean. Arrange asparagus spears spoke fashion on top of quiche. Place cherry tomato halves in between the spokes.
Yield: 6 to 8 servings

## Hope-Bosworth House

The Bosworth family has been in this country for a very long time. They came from England on one of the ships that sailed with the Mayflower. George M. Bosworth was a prominent business man in Geyserville, California in the late 1800's. He owned the mercantile store, the funeral parlor, the cemetery and the waterworks. In 1904 he built a large Queen Anne style home for his family on Geyserville Avenue.

The architect's plan for the home was called a "pattern book house" and was purchased from the Sears catalogue. The house was built with day labor and all the milling for the custom shiplap siding was done on site under the direction of Mr. Bosworth. The house was made of redwood except for the floors and woodwork that are of oak. The wallpaper in one of the rooms is a reproduction of William Morris design.

The Bosworth family lived in the home until the middle 1960's. In 1980, the Hopes purchased the home and made some changes in converting it into a bed and breakfast.

Ron and Cosette Scheiber left San Jose, California to purchase and operate the Hope-Bosworth and the Hope-Merrill House Inns. The two Inns are run as one entity. The guests at the Hope-Bosworth generally have their breakfast in the dining room of the Hope-Merrill House. If there are a large number of guests, the gourmet breakfast is delivered to the Hope-Bosworth House.

The Hope-Bosworth House is in the wine country. Ron and Cosette decided to provide the wine making experience for their guests. The event is done in two parts. The first two and one half days stay includes the picking and pressing of the grapes under the supervision of Graham Parnell. Mr. Parnell is the Chairman of the West Coast Wine Competition and co-coordinator of the grand Harvest Awards Competition. He has been the Pick and Press winemaker for the Scheiber's for the past 14 years. The following spring the guests return for the taste, blend, bottling and labeling of the wine. Each guest takes home two cases of "their" wine.

Cosette told me she learned to cook from her father-in-law back in the 1950's when French cuisine was popular. She has adjusted her menus to a more California style taste. Ron also enjoys cooking. They are excellent cooks as you will find as you prepare and enjoy their recipes.

## American Red Velvet Cake

1 1/2 cups sugar
1/2 cup unsalted butter, softened
2 large eggs
2 1/4 cups sifted cake flour
2 teaspoons cocoa powder
1 teaspoon baking soda
1 teaspoon baking powder
1 teaspoon salt
1 cup buttermilk
1/4 teaspoon red food coloring
1 teaspoon distilled white vinegar
1 teaspoon vanilla

❖ *This cake is also known as the Waldorf Astoria Red Cake. The story behind this cake is that a lady dining at the Waldorf Austoria Hotel in New York enjoyed this cake so much that upon her return home she wrote to the pastry chef asking for the recipe. She said she would be happy to pay for the recipe. The recipe arrived, along with a bill for $10,000! The story states that she did indeed have to pay for the recipe. She then generously gave the recipe to everyone she knew.*

Preheat oven to 350 degrees. In large mixing bowl cream sugar and butter. Beat in eggs, one at a time. In separate bowl combine flour, cocoa, baking soda, baking powder and salt. Add dry ingredients alternately with buttermilk to creamed mixture. Add red food coloring, vinegar and vanilla, beating to blend. Spread batter into 9-inch greased and floured cake pans. Bake for 20 minutes at 350 degrees. Remove from oven and cool on rack. Place 1 layer on cake plate. Frost and cover with second layer. Frost top and sides of cake.
Yield: 12 to 16 servings

### Cake Frosting

1/2 cup unsalted butter or margarine, softened
1 package (8 ounces) cream cheese, softened
1 pound powdered sugar
1 teaspoon vanilla
1/2 cup pecans, chopped

In mixing bowl, cream butter and cream cheese. Add sugar and beat until fluffy. Add vanilla. Beat. Add pecans and mix.

## Decadent Fudge Cake

1 cup butter or margarine, softened
1 1/2 cups sugar
4 eggs
1/2 teaspoon baking soda
1 cup buttermilk
2 1/2 cups all-purpose flour
1 1/2 cups semi-sweet chocolate mini-morsels, divided
2 bars (4 ounces) sweet baking chocolate
1/3 cup chocolate syrup
2 teaspoons vanilla
4 ounces white chocolate, chopped
2 tablespoons plus 2 teaspoons shortening
Chocolate and white chocolate leaves

❖ *Add buttermilk alternately with flour, starting with flour and ending with flour.*

❖ *Do not over beat.*

❖ *Cake is done when it springs back after gently touched.*

❖ *Suggested wine pairings-*
  *Late Harvest Zinfandel*
  *Ruby Port*

Preheat oven to 300 degrees. In mixing bowl cream butter, gradually add sugar, beating well at medium speed. Add eggs, one at a time, beating after each addition. Dissolve soda in buttermilk, Mix well. Add to creamed mixture alternately with four additions of flour. Add 1 cup mini-morsels, melted chocolate, chocolate syrup and vanilla, stirring just until blended. Spoon batter into heavily greased and floured 10 inch bundt pan. Bake for 85 to 95 minutes at 300 degrees. Invert cake immediately onto serving plate. Let cool completely. In top of double boiler combine 4 ounces white chocolate and 2 tablespoon shortening. Bring water to a boil. Reduce heat to low, cook until mixture is melted and smooth. Remove from heat. Drizzle melted white chocolate mixture over cake. Melt remaining 1/2 cup mini-morsels and 2 teaspoons shortening in small sauce pan over low heat, stirring until smooth. Remove from heat. Cool completely. Drizzle over white chocolate on cake.
Yield: 12 to 16 servings

## Breakfast Bread Pudding

2 eggs
3/4 cup sugar
4 cups half and half cream
1/2 cup unsalted butter, melted
1 tablespoon vanilla
3/4 cup dried currants or raisins
1 teaspoon nutmeg
1 loaf baguette bread, sliced 2 inches thick

❖ *Serve with warm berry sauce.*

❖ *Sprinkle top of pudding with powdered sugar before serving.*

Preheat oven to 350 degrees. Combine all ingredients except bread. Place bread slices in large bowl. Pour egg mixture over bread. Let stand for 20 minutes. Arrange bread slices in lightly greased 4 quart baking dish. Pour remaining egg mixture over bread. Bake uncovered for 45 minutes at 350 degrees, until custard is set and pudding is lightly brown.
Yield: 8 servings

## Warm Berry Sauce

2 cups fresh or frozen raspberries
2 cups fresh or frozen strawberries
1/3 cup sugar
1/3 cup orange juice, fresh squeezed
3 tablespoons lemon juice

❖ *Warm berry sauce can be served on ice cream or custard.*

In sauce pan combine all ingredients. Cook over medium heat, stirring constantly, until fruit begins to break up, about 5 minutes. Puree in food processor or blender. Return to sauce pan and heat until warm. Serve with bread pudding
Yield: 4 1/2 cups

*Hope-Merrill House*

The Hope-Merrill house was built by J. P. Merrill and his wife Martha in 1870. The Eastlake stick style Victorian architecture was popular between 1870 and 1885. Mr. Merrill was a land developer and a lumber baron. He used the local redwood lumber to build this beautiful home and has quarter-sawn oak in all doors and woodwork.

The home was sold in 1950 and remodeled. In the ensuing years it became a convalescent home and then was divided into apartments.

In 1980, the Hopes bought the property and set about restoring it to its original grandeur. This was a mammoth job and took 4 years. During the reconstruction Rosalie Hope found architectural treasures when the false ceiling was removed. This allowed her to replace the bay window, the pocket doors and the large front windows. When completed the home became a bed and breakfast.

As I traveled around Northern California visiting bed and breakfasts I found that each are unique in some way. The Hope-Merrill House Inn in Geyserville has the most unique, beautiful wallpaper. Art buffs and designers would describe this as a gold mine. In the middle 1800's William Morris was known world wide for his elaborate wallpaper designs. The rolls of beautifully crafted paper were shipped from England around the world. Rosalie Hope, the new owner of the Hope-

Merrill House in 1980 met with Bruce Bradbary, a talented silk screen artist, who made exact reproductions of William Morris's wallpaper. Bruce Bradbary designed the wallpaper throughout the entire Hope-Merrill house. The wallpaper in the dining room was designed to match the Rosalie Masion china from England. This china is now made by Spode and the pattern is still available. The front hallway paper is exclusive to this house. The guest room on the first floor has bold colors in the wallpaper. The frieze around the top of the walls features the stylized peacocks of William Morris, beautifully reproduced by Mr. Bradbary.

Another unique feature of the home is the original Lincrusta-Walton wainscoting found in the downstairs entrance and upstairs hallway. Lincrusta, originally composed of wood fiber and various chemicals became the rage in the 1880's when a decorator got the idea of embossing floor linoleum and putting it on walls.

Ron and Cosette Scheiber purchased this home and the Hope-Bosworth house across the street to operate as a joint bed and breakfast. They were well acquainted with bed and breakfasts after 20 years of exploring bed and breakfasts around the United States and in Europe.

# Baked Eggs and Potatoes

1/4 cup (1/2 stick) butter
1/4 cup all-purpose flour
2 cups milk
1 1/4 teaspoons salt
1 1/2 teaspoons chili powder
1 1/2 teaspoons garlic, minced
1 1/2 teaspoons freshly ground pepper
5 medium red potatoes
1 tablespoon salt
1 medium red bell pepper, diced
1/2 teaspoon vegetable oil
12 eggs
1 tablespoon baking powder
2 cups cheddar cheese, grated

❖ *Creole seasoning can be substituted for chili powder.*

❖ *Serve with sour cream and salsa.*

❖ *Suggested wine pairing - Blanc de Blanc Champagne*

In large sauce pan melt butter. Add flour and cook over low heat for 5 minutes. Slowly add milk, beating with wire whip. Add salt, chili powder, garlic and black pepper. Simmer until mixture begins to thicken. Refrigerate over night. Boil potatoes with 1 tablespoon salt, until soft but firm, about 30 minutes. Cool. Cut into 1/2 inch cubes. Refrigerate over night. Sauté red pepper in 1/2 teaspoon oil, until slightly soft. Drain liquid from pan. Refrigerate peppers overnight. In morning, preheat oven to 325 degrees. In large mixing bowl beat eggs. Add peppers, potatoes, baking powder, white sauce and cheese. Mix well. Pour mixture into greased baking dish. Bake for 40 minutes at 325 degrees.
Yield: 8 servings

## Legume Soup

Equal amounts of:
small white beans, red beans, pinto beans, black beans, pearl barley,
lentils, black eyed peas, green and yellow split peas.
3 ham hocks
1 large onion, chopped
1 green bell pepper, chopped
3 stalks celery, chopped
1 can (28 ounces) whole tomatoes
2 cloves garlic, minced
Juice of 1 lemon
1 teaspoon sugar
Salt and pepper to taste
1 cup sausage or ground beef, cooked, drained

❖ *Not all beans are necessary for the soup. The amount used can vary.*

❖ *Watch level of liquid because beans soak up a lot of the liquid.*

Wash and soak beans overnight. Drain. Place in a large pot. Cover with water. Add ham hocks. Simmer for 2 1/2 hours. Add remaining ingredients, except ground meat. Simmer for 30 minutes. Add meat and simmer to warm.
Yield: approximately 1 gallon, varies with amount of beans used

❖ *Suggested wine pairing - Cream Sherry*

## Baked Eggs with Artichokes

1 tablespoon unsalted butter, softened
2 teaspoons fresh chives, chopped
1 teaspoon fresh parsley, chopped
1 teaspoon fresh oregano, chopped
8 canned artichoke hearts, quartered, drained
2 large eggs
Salt and pepper, as desired
2 tablespoons parmesan cheese, grated

❖ *Do not break yolk.*

❖ *Serve eggs immediately.*

Preheat oven to 400 degrees. Rub butter onto bottom and sides of two 3/4 cup souffle dishes or custard cups. Sprinkle chives, parsley and oregano evenly in dishes. Place 4 artichoke hearts into each dish. Crack egg into each dish. Sprinkle eggs with salt, pepper and cheese. Cover. Bake about 9 minutes at 400 degrees until eggs are softly set and cheese is golden.
Yield: 2 servings

## Breakfast Sausage with Sliced Pineapple

30 breakfast pork sausage links
1 can (16 ounces) pineapple slices, including juice

❖ *For many years the Scheiber family began their Saturday mornings aboard their sailboat with a delicious breakfast that included this wonderful sausage dish.*

❖ *Turn pork links while they are cooking.*

❖ *Make sure not to reduce juices so much that the links begin to burn.*

Place pork links in heavy skillet. Pour half of pineapple juice on links. Sauté over medium heat. Remove from skilled when links are brown. Add pineapple slices and glaze in pan juices. Add glazed pineapple to pork links.
Yield: 6 to 8 servings

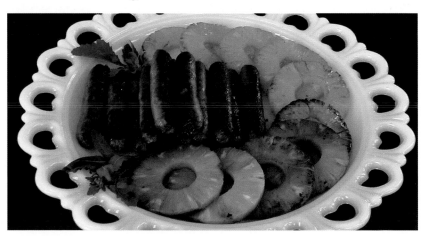

# Directory of Northern California Inns

**FOOTHILL HOUSE**
3037 Foothill Blvd.
Calistoga, CA 94515
800-942-6933
707-942-6933
info@foothillhouse.com
Darla Anderson

**BEAR FLAG INN**
2653 Foothill Blvd.
Calistoga, CA 94515
800-670-2860
707-942-5534
dennismcnay@sbcglobal.net
Marge and Dennis McNay

**CHELSEA GARDEN INN**
1443 Second Street
Calistoga, CA 94515
800-942-1515
707-942-0948
innkeeper@chelseagardeninn.com
Dave and Susan DeVries

**BRANNAN COTTAGE INN**
109 Wapoo Avenue
Calistoga, CA 94515
707-942-4200
brannancottageinn@sbcgloal.net
Doug and Judy Cook

**ADAGIO INN**
1417 Kearney Street
St. Helena, CA 94574
888-08ADAGIO
707-963-2238
innkeeper@adagioinn.com
Polly Keegan

**WINE COUNTRY INN**
1152 Lodi Lane
St. Helena, CA 94574
888-465-4608
707-963-7077
jim@winecountryinn.com
Jim Smith

**MAISON FLEURIE**
6529 Yount Street
Yountville, CA 94599
800-788-0369
707-944-2056
maisonfleurienapa.com
Four Sisters Inns

**LAVENDER**
2020 Webber Avenue
Yountville, CA 94599
800-522-4140
707-944-1388
lavendernapa.com
Four Sisters Inns

**BLACKBIRD INN**
1755 First Street
Napa, CA 94559
888-567-9811
707-226-2450
blackbirdinnnapa.com
Four Sisters Inns

**HENNESSEY HOUSE INN**
1727 Main Street
Napa, CA 94559
800-371-8012
707-226-3774
hennesseyhousebedandbrekfast.com
Lorri and Kevin Walsh

# Directory of Northern California Inns

**BEAZLEY HOUSE**
1910 First Street
Napa, CA 94559
888-559-1649
707-257-1649
innkeeper@beazleyhouse.com
Carol and Jim Beazley

**DAUGHTERS INN**
1938 First Street
Napa, CA 94559
866-253-1331
707-253-1331
carol@daughtersinn.com
Carol and Jim Beazley

**NAPA INN**
1137 Warren Street
Napa, CA 94559
800-435-1144
707-257-1444
napainn.com
Brooke Boyer

**BUFORD HOUSE INN**
920 Clay Street
Napa, CA 94559
800-435-1144
707-257-1444
napainn.com
Brooke Boyer

**HIDDEN OAK INN**
214 East Napa Street
Sonoma, CA 95476
877-996-9863
707-996-9863
hiddenoakinn.com
Valerie Patterson

**THISTLE DEW INN**
171 West Spain Street
Sonoma, CA 95476
800-382-7895
707-938-2909
info@thistledew.com
Jan Rafiq and Gregg Percival

**A CAPTAIN'S HOUSE**
At Larson Family Winery
23355 Millerick Road
Sonoma, CA 95476
707-938-3031
becky@larsonfamilywinery.com
Becky Larson

**TROJAN HORSE INN**
19455 Sonoma Highway
Sonoma CA 95476
800-899-1925
707-996-2430
trojanhorseinn.com
Bethany Johns

**BELTANE RANCH**
P.O. Box 395 / 11775 Sonoma Highway
Glen Ellen, CA 95442
707-833-4233
707-996-6501
anne@beltaneranch.com
Alexa Wood

**CASE RANCH INN**
7446 Poplar Drive
Forestville, CA 95436
877-887-8711
707-887-8711
Diana@caseranchinn.com
Diana Van Ry

# Directory of Northern California Inns

**AVALON**
11991 Graton Road
Sebastopol, CA 95472
877-328-2566
707-824-0880
avalonluxuryinn.com
Hilary McCalla

**RAFORD INN**
10630 Wohler Road
Healdsburg, CA 95448
800-887-9503
707-887-9573
rafordinn.com
Rita Wells

**HEALDSBURG INN ON THE PLAZA**
112 Matheson Street
Healdsburg, CA 95448
800-431-8663
707-433-6991
healdsburginn.com
Four Sisters Inns

**CREEKSIDE INN AND RESORT**
P.O. Box 2185 / 16180 Neely Road
Guerneville, CA 95446
800-776-6586
707-869-3623
stay@creeeksideinn.com
creeksideinn.com
Lynn Crescione

**VILLAGE INN & RESTAURANT**
20822 River Boulevard
Monte Rio, CA 95462
800-303-2303
707-865-2304
village@sonic.net
Mark Bethumeur

**SONOMA COAST VILLA INN & SPA**
16702 Highway One
Bodega, CA. 94922
888-404-2255
707-876-9818
reservations@scvilla.com
Johannes C. Zaehbauer

**NORTH COAST COUNTRY INN**
34591 South Highway One
Gualala, CA 95445
800-959-4537
707-884-4537
nccinn@gmail.com
Sandy and Phil Walker

**ELK COVE INN & SPA**
6300 South Highway One
P.O. Box 367
Elk, CA 95432
800-275-2967
707-877-3321
innkeeper@elkcoveinn.com
David Lieberman

**STEVENSWOOD RESORT & SPA**
8211 North Highway One
Mendocino, CA. 95456
800-421-2810
707-937-2810
stevenswood.com
Seth Kelman
Michael Webster

# Directory of Northern California Inns

**AGATE COVE INN**
11201 North Lansing Street
P.O. Box 1150
Mendocino, CA. 95460
800-527-3111
707-937-0551
info@agatecove.com
Laraine Galloway

**THE WHITEGATE INN**
499 Howard Street
P.O. Box 150
Mendocino, CA. 95460
800-531-7282
707-937-4892
whitegateinn.com
Richard Strom

**JOSHUA GRINDLE INN**
44800 Little Lake Road
P.O. Box 647
Mendocino, CA 95460
800-grindle
707-937-4143
joshugrin.com
Charles Reinhart

**THE WELLER HOUSE INN**
524 Stewart Street
Fort Bragg, CA 95437
877-893-5537
707-964-4415
ted@wellerhouse.com
Ted and Eva Kidwell

**HOPE-BOSWORTH HOUSE**
21238 Geyserville Avenue
Geyserville, CA 95441
800-825-4233
707-857-3350
hope-inns.com
Ron and Cosette Scheiber

**HOPE-MERRILL HOUSE**
21253 Geyserville Avenue
Geyserville, CA 95441
800-825-4233
707-857-3350
hope-inns.com
Ron and Cosette Scheiber

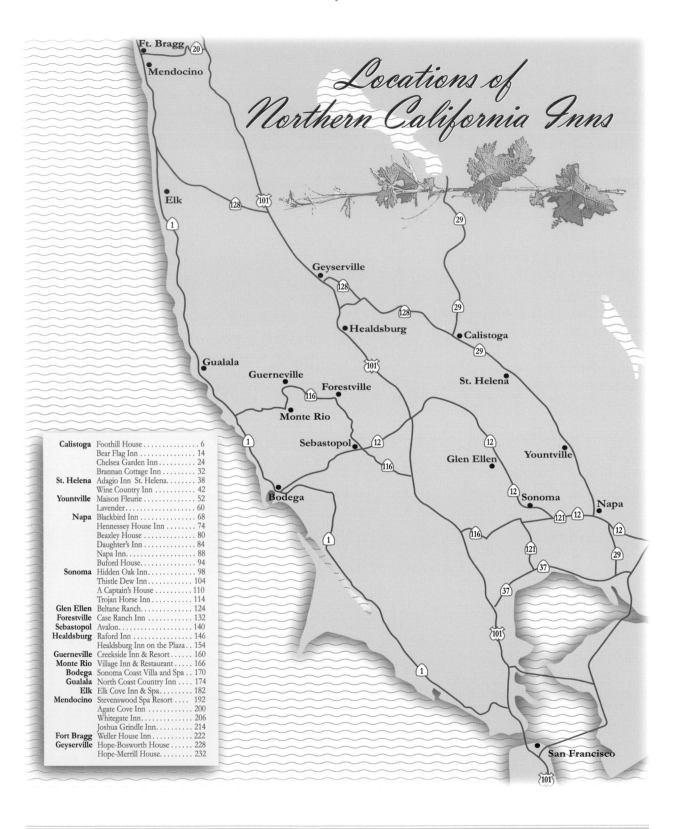

# Locations of Northern California Inns

# Recipe Index

# Recipe Index

# Recipe Index

# Recipe Index

# Recipe Index

# *Recipe Index*

# Recipe Index

# Recipe Index

# *Recipe Index*

# Recipe Index

# *Recipe Index*

# Recipe Index